THIS MINUTE, THIS WEEK, THIS MONTH

THE FINANCIAL DISCIPLINE SYSTEM FOR MEN

MATTHEW BLACK

The Financial Discipline System for Men

This Minute, This Week, This Month

ISBN # **979-8-9942332-1-4**

Published by FWS Investments

Fws@FwsInvestments.com

FINANCIAL DISCLAIMER AND LIMITATION OF LIABILITY

This book is published for general informational and educational purposes only. The author, Matthew Black, is not a licensed financial advisor, investment advisor, accountant, attorney, or other regulated financial or legal professional. Nothing in this publication constitutes financial advice, investment advice, legal advice, tax advice, or any other form of professional advice regulated by law.

The strategies, methods, frameworks, and suggestions presented in this book reflect the author's personal experience and research. They are offered as general educational content and are not tailored to the financial circumstances, goals, risk tolerance, or legal situation of any individual reader.

Past results described in this book are not a guarantee, promise, or prediction of future results. Financial outcomes depend on individual circumstances, economic conditions, and a wide range of factors outside the author's knowledge or control. Results will vary.

Readers are strongly encouraged to consult a qualified and licensed financial advisor, tax professional, or attorney before making financial decisions of any kind, including but not limited to: debt management, retirement planning, investment strategy, insurance, estate planning, or any major change to personal financial arrangements.

The author and publisher make no representations or warranties of any kind, express or implied, regarding the completeness, accuracy, reliability, suitability, or availability of the information contained in this book. Any reliance you place on such information is strictly at your own risk.

To the fullest extent permitted by applicable law, the author and publisher disclaim all liability for any loss, damage, cost, or expense—whether direct, indirect, incidental,

MEDICAL AND HEALTH DISCLAIMER

This publication is not intended as a substitute for professional medical or psychological advice. The author is not a licensed health professional. Nothing in this book should be construed as medical, psychological, or therapeutic guidance. Consult a qualified healthcare provider regarding any health-related concerns.

Printed in the United States of America.

❀ Formatted with Vellum

INTRODUCTION

You don't know me. That's fine. You don't need to.

What you need to know is this: I spent twenty years studying the martial arts and another decade in security operations where mistakes were unforgiving. And somewhere in that training and doing—on the mats, in the ring, in situations where hesitation meant catastrophic failure—I learned something that changed my entire financial life.

The same principles that work in combat work with money. Actual tactical principles that produce real results. The martial arts teach more than battle theory—they teach a discipline that transfers to all that you do in this life.

I applied those principles religiously. I closed gaps. I built buffers. I eliminated debt. I attacked every financial battle the same way I was taught to approach a real fight: observe the situation clearly, orient to what it means, decide on the next move, and execute immediately.

The result? I retired early. Not through luck or a fat family inheritance. Not through some massive income. Through consistent action of combat principles applied to money over years of disciplined practice. I secured my position first, then I built the foundation that gives me the freedom to focus on what matters instead of scrambling to survive.

That's what this book teaches you to do.

I'm not a financial advisor. I'm not a certified planner. I'm not selling courses or coaching programs. I'm a lifelong martial arts practitioner who applied martial discipline to money and got results—and I'm going to show you exactly how I did it so you can do the same.

The wisdom isn't mine. It comes from warriors who've been teaching these principles for centuries. Musashi. Sun Tzu. Col. Boyd. Men who understood that the same mindset that wins fights wins every other battle in life, including the financial one.

You're reading this because you're in that place right now. Running those calculations. Carrying that weight. Fighting that fight alone.

And the fact that you're here, reading this, looking for a way through —means you haven't given up. That matters more than you know.

This isn't motivational speaking or rah-rah inspiration nonsense. This is tactical instruction from someone who walked the path and can show you the exact framework that will do the job.

The question isn't whether the SOP works. It does. The question is whether you'll do it.

So here's what's about to happen. I'm going to show you the enemy you're actually fighting—not money problems, but paralysis. Then I'm going to walk you through every battle: the emergency fund you don't have, the monthly gap bleeding you dry, the debt trap, the retirement impossibility, the fragility, the isolation. For each battle, you get three tools: what to do this minute, this week, and this month.

Do all of it religiously, and you'll be standing where I'm standing: debt-free, buffer built, retirement secured, position unbreakable.

I can show you the path. I can give you the SOP. But I can't make you take the first step. Only you can do that.

So let's get started.

- Matthew Black

PREFACE

I've watched men carry weight in silence their whole lives.

Men who showed up. Did the work. Kept the lights on. Never missed a shift, never asked for help, never let anyone see how close to the edge the math had gotten.

And I've watched that silence cost them.

Not in dramatic ways. Not usually. More often in the slow erosion of a man who started out with plans and ended up just managing. Who stopped dreaming about building something and started hoping nothing breaks. Who learned to answer "are we okay?" with "we're fine"—and got *so good* at saying it that he almost believed it.

I wrote this book because I kept having the same conversation.

Different men. Different numbers. Same fight. Emergency with no buffer. Month that doesn't close. Debt that doesn't move. Retirement account that's technically there but also effectively doesn't exist. And beneath all of it, the part nobody talks about—the weight of carrying it alone. The specific shame of being a provider who's struggling to provide.

Every time I had that conversation, I gave the same framework. The same sequence. The same tools. And every time, it worked — not because it's complicated, but because it isn't. Because the principles that produce results in a training environment produce results in a financial one. Because discipline applied consistently over time wins. Every time.

It's time to stop having the same conversation one person at a time.

That's this book.

If you're in that fight—if you're the man running calculations at 3 AM that never quite add up—this book is written for you. Not around you. For you.

The path through exists. You're holding it.

CHAPTER 1
FREE MONEY

"First learn stand, then learn fly. Nature rule, Daniel-san, not mine"

- Mr. Miyagi

Can I ask you a question? And I want you to answer it quickly and honestly. Not what you think you should say. What you actually think.

If I walked up to you right now and handed you a significant sum of money—enough that it feels like it would solve your problems, 50 grand, 150 grand, ten million, cash, no strings attached, no taxes taken out, just yours to keep—would that actually solve your money problems?

Really think about it for a second.

CHAPTER 1

What's your gut telling you?

Maybe your gut is saying yes. Absolutely yes. That money would pay off the credit cards. Maybe build up some savings for once. Catch up on all the little things you're behind on. Finally be able to breathe. Maybe for the first time in years.

Or maybe your number is different. Maybe you're thinking less would do it. Or maybe you need more.

The exact amount doesn't matter.

What matters is this: somewhere in your head, you believe that a certain amount of money would fix your situation. That if you just had that amount, your world would be okay.

What I say next might be hard to hear.

That money won't fix your problems.

And I can prove it to you.

WHEN MONEY DOESN'T FIX ANYTHING

I will present to you the story about a guy named Jack Whittaker.

In 2002—this is a true story—Jack won the Powerball lottery. Not just any lottery. The biggest single jackpot in U.S. history at that time. Three hundred and fifteen million dollars.

Think about that for a second. $315 million.

That's more money than most people could spend in ten lifetimes.

So what happened to Jack?

Four years later, he was broke. Completely broke.

But it gets worse. His granddaughter died from a drug overdose. His daughter died shortly after that. His wife left him. People kept robbing him because they knew he had money. People kept suing him. He started drinking himself to death in bars. He'd pull out hundred—dollar bills and dare people to try to take them from him.

In 2020, Jack Whittaker died broken and alone.

You know what he told reporters years before he died? He said, "I wish I'd torn that ticket up."

Three hundred and fifteen million dollars. All of it gone.

Now, you might be thinking: "Well, that's just one guy. He obviously didn't know how to handle money."

Okay. Want more proof?

Seventy eight percent, —that's more than three out of every four—NFL players go bankrupt or have serious money trouble within two years of retiring. Bankrupt means you officially tell the government you have no money left and can't pay what you owe. Just two years after they stop playing football.

Sixty percent of NBA players go broke within five years of leaving the league.

These aren't dumb people. These are men who made millions of dollars playing professional sports. Ten million. Twenty million. Fifty million in their careers.

And they had help. All the usual suspects. They had financial advisors, people whose whole job is helping you manage investments. They had accountants, lots of bean counters. People who do nothing but handle money for a living. They had agents and managers. They had professionals and "smart people" telling them what to do.

And they still lost it all.

Mike Tyson—you've probably heard of him, the boxer—made hundreds of millions in the ring. He ended up filing for bankruptcy.

Professional basketball and football players who earned over $100 million in their careers. Bankrupt.

A boxer who earned over $200 million. Lost every penny.

Here's my question: if the problem was just not having enough money, why did all these extremely successful people lose it after they had made so much?

The answer is simple:

The problem wasn't the amount of money they had. The problem was their system—the way they thought about money and handled it—couldn't hold what they had.

Their operating system for handling money was barely designed for making fifty thousand a year, let alone five million a year. What do I mean? An operating system is the automatic way your brain runs something without thinking.

Picture brushing your teeth: you don't decide "okay, toothbrush in right hand, toothpaste on brush, brush top teeth first, then bottom teeth, thirty seconds each quadrant." You just brush. Your brain runs the program automatically. That's your operating system for brushing teeth.

Same thing with money. You have an automatic system running right now. Get paid → pay bills → spend whatever's left → hope something's left for savings → usually nothing is. That system runs automatically every month. You're not deciding to do it that way. It's just happening.

So when the money showed up, their system couldn't hold it.

It's like trying to carry water in a fishing net. Doesn't matter how much water you pour in. It's all going to run right back out through the holes.

WHY YOUR SYSTEM HAS HOLES

The holes in your financial system aren't there by accident.

They were designed. Deliberately. By people way smarter than you and me.

You're not struggling because you're bad with money. You're struggling because you're under attack. Constant, sophisticated, psychological attack.

Every day, from the moment you wake up until you go to sleep, you're being told who you should be. What you should own. What you should look like. What you should drive. Where you should vacation.

The marketing isn't amateur hour. The companies behind it aren't guessing.

They employ behavioral psychologists. Neuroscientists. People who understand exactly how your brain makes decisions and exactly how to hijack those decisions.

Edward Bernays, the father of modern public relations and propaganda, wrote the playbook for this a century ago. He called it "engineering consent." Taking what people want and making them think they need what you're selling instead.

They've been refining that playbook for a hundred years. They have your data. Your browsing history. Your purchase patterns. Your weaknesses. They know what triggers you before you do.

And they use all of it to create holes in your system. Holes that money leaks through.

This isn't some conspiracy theory. This is their business model. Your financial stress is their profit center. Every dollar you mismanage, is a dollar that flows to someone who understands this game better than you do.

You're not failing to properly manage your money. You're losing a psychological war you didn't know you were fighting.

But now you know.

WHAT WOULD REALLY HAPPEN TO YOU

I'll walk you through what would actually happen if I gave you your magic number right now. Whatever amount you think would solve all your problems.

You'd pay off the debt. That's smart. I'm not saying it's not smart.

You'd put some money aside for emergencies. Also smart.

Then what?

Well, you'd loosen up a little bit. Right? And you should. You've been stressed for years. You've been grinding. Working hard. Trying to make ends meet. You deserve to breathe a little.

Maybe you take the family on that vacation you've been putting off. Nothing crazy. Just a normal vacation unwinding on a beach at a cheap all-inclusive resort.

Maybe you finally buy that work truck you've been needing. Or maybe just a more reliable car. Something that won't break down every other month.

Maybe you say yes when your kid asks about joining the sports travel team. Or the dance class. Or whatever thing they've been wanting to do that you've had to say no to because you couldn't afford it.

Nothing crazy, or outrageous. Just normal stuff.

Six months go by.

That emergency money you set aside? It's starting to look smaller. Because an unexpected expense hit. The kind that always hits. And you had to pull some money out to cover it. You tell yourself you'll put it back. But you don't.

Life keeps costing money. And the regular expenses—the baseline stuff you have to pay every month—those are creeping up. Because you're not being as careful anymore. You're not watching every single dollar like you used to. You have a cushion now. You can afford to relax a little bit.

Twelve months go by.

You check the account. The cushion is a lot thinner than you thought it would be. Some of the debt is back. Not all of it. Not as much as before. But enough that you notice it. You're not in crisis mode. But you're not in the clear either.

Eighteen months go by.

You're back where you started. Maybe not as deep in the hole. But the same pattern. The same stress. The same gap—when your expenses are more than your income— that space between what you earn and what you spend—between what comes in and what goes out.

Let's pretend you make $3,400 a month. Your bills, food, gas, all that adds up to $3,600. That's a $200 gap. Every single month, you're $200 short. That's the gap between what comes in and what goes out. Same gap. Same stress. Same waking up at three in the morning doing math in your head.

What happened?

The money didn't change your system. Your system absorbed that money and went right back to how it was before.

Like a sponge. Pour water on a sponge and it swells up. But then it dries out and shrinks right back to its original shape.

This isn't me judging you. I'm not saying you're bad with money. I'm saying there's a system running underneath how you handle money. And unless you change that system, more money just flows through it and disappears.

That's physics. That's how systems work.

THE REAL PROBLEM ISN'T HOW MUCH YOU MAKE

Here's a number that might surprise you: Forty—two percent, almost half, of people making $100,000 a year or more—that's people making six figures or more are living paycheck to paycheck. If you didn't know, that means you run out of money before you run out of month. Your next paycheck barely shows up in time to cover what you owe. Six figures? Almost half? Broke? Yes, it's true, and that is not really hard to imagine why. It is the system they are running. The way they are thinking about the information they have and the automatic reactive decisions they make with it, because of their subconscious programming.

I've known guys doing mall security work making $35,000 a year who retired millionaires. And I've known dentists making $200,000 a year who couldn't make rent at sixty five.

The difference wasn't intelligence. Wasn't work ethic. And it certainly wasn't luck.

It was their system. One guy had a system that held money. The other guy had a system that leaked it.

That's what we're really talking about here. Not your income. Your system.

Your system isn't broken by accident. You are in a game. You were not told about the game, or how it's played. You were set loose with no information and no plan, no warning of the sharks in the waters you would be navigating.

Think about your current position this way: You're sitting at a poker table right now. Whether you know it or not, you've been sitting there for years. And the old adage goes, if you look around the table and can't spot the sucker—you're the sucker.

The game is rigged. Not obviously rigged like a back—alley dice game. Rigged in the cleverest ways. Three card monte clever. Shell game clever. The kind where you're watching the cups move, swearing you saw which one has the ball, betting all you have—and losing every single time.

You think you're making free choices about where your money goes. You're not. You're operating in a carefully choreographed con, and you've been the mark since the first credit card offer showed up in your mailbox.

Your system isn't just broken. It's under attack. Sophisticated attack. Coordinated attack. Psychological attack designed by people who've spent decades figuring out exactly how to separate you from your money before you even realize it's gone.

The house always wins. And you're not the house.

TIME TO MEET YOUR OPPONENTS

Right now, as you're reading this, five forces are working against your system. Think of them as five opponents. You're in the ring with all five at once. They don't take turns. You are outnumbered and getting hit from all sides, and the blows are coming in fast.

Most providers don't even know they're fighting. They just feel the stress. The weight. The constant pressure that something's wrong but they can't name what it is.

I'm going to name them for you.

Once you can see them, you can fight them. But you can't fight what you can't see.

These are your five opponents, and they're attacking you right now.

OPPONENT 1: *DESIRE*

The initial opponent doesn't look like an enemy.

Desire moves smooth. Attractive. Seductive.

Makes you feel poor when you're not. Makes you feel like you're falling behind when you're not. Makes every choice feel like choosing between living fully and just surviving.

The new truck. The nicer house. The vacation everyone's posting about. The lifestyle that signals you've made it.

Desire doesn't force you. Doesn't have to. Just keeps circling, showing you what you could have right now, making waiting feel like losing.

Desire is dangerous for providers specifically: you've earned it. You actually have. You went to school. You work hard. You help people. You deserve nice things. You deserve a comfortable life.

And *Desire* knows that. Uses it against you.

Every advertisement you see. Every social media post. Every conversation with colleagues who just bought something new. *Desire* is there whispering: "You work harder than they do. You should have what they have."

It's not wrong. But it's not the whole truth either.

The whole truth is this: every dollar *Desire* convinces you to spend today is a dollar that can't work for you tomorrow. And the stress you feel? A lot of it comes from trying to afford a lifestyle *Desire* sold you instead of the lifestyle your current system can actually hold.

OPPONENT 2: *DISTRACTION*

Second opponent is a magician.

Distraction doesn't hit you directly. Creates complexity instead. Overwhelms you with options. Makes little problems feel urgent when they aren't. A constant state of crisis that will lead to mental fatigue and hopelessness.

Seventeen different utilities and monthly billing accounts. Three streaming services you forgot you're paying for. Credit cards with interest rates and rewards programs that require spreadsheets to understand. Insurance policies you signed but never read. Subscriptions auto renewing for things you used once. It's mind numbing to sit down and review the entire jumble.

Distraction makes your financial life so complicated that managing it becomes a second job. A job you don't have time for because you already have a job. So you don't manage it. You just let it run. And it runs you into the ground.

For providers, *Distraction* is especially brutal because your real job is already cognitively demanding. You're making hard calls all day. Managing competing priorities. Dealing with pressure that doesn't let up.

By the time you get home, your decision making capacity is depleted. That's when *Distraction* attacks. When you're too tired to think clearly. When you just want things to be simple but it all seems so complicated and blurred.

And the stress builds. Because somewhere in your gut you know you should be handling this stuff. Confidently on top of it. But you're not. And you feel it.

OPPONENT 3: *COMPARISON*

Third opponent carries a mirror.

Comparison shows you everyone else's highlight reel. Their new car. Their vacation photos. Their bigger house. Their promotions. Their success. Social media envy as you scroll through seeing what seems to be a perfect life, certainly better than yours.

Photos never shows you their debt, or their fights about money. Their stress. The reality behind the image.

Comparison makes you measure your life against carefully curated performances. Makes you feel like you're losing a race you didn't even know you were running.

Comparison is particularly toxic for providers: you're surrounded by other high earners. Other professionals. People who look successful. And you assume they have it figured out.

They don't.

Remember that stat I gave you? Forty two percent of people making over $100,000 live paycheck to paycheck. Some of those people are your colleagues. Your friends. The people whose lives you're comparing yourself to.

But you don't see their bank accounts. You see their stuff.

So you stress about why you can't afford what they can afford. Why you're struggling when they seem fine. Why your system isn't working when theirs appears to be.

The truth? Their system probably isn't working either. They're just better at hiding it. Or they're deeper in debt. Or they're one emergency away from collapse.

Comparison steals your peace and gives you nothing in return.

OPPONENT 4: *FEAR*

Fourth opponent whispers.

Fear doesn't tell you to act. Tells you to wait. To research more. To be certain before you move. To avoid mistakes at all costs.

Fear points at every risk. Every way things could go wrong. Every story about someone who tried and failed. Every reason why now isn't the right time.

Fear creates paralysis disguised as prudence.

For providers, *Fear* speaks in professional language. Sounds rational:

"What if I need that money for an emergency?"

"What if I make the wrong choice and lose my shirt?"

"What if the economy crashes right after I invest?"

"What if I can't keep up the savings rate?"

"What if I'm doing this wrong?"

These aren't stupid questions. They're legitimate concerns. But *Fear* uses legitimate concerns to prevent any action at all.

And here's the trap: inaction feels safe. Feels responsible. Feels like you're being smart by waiting.

But inaction is still a choice. And that choice has consequences. Every month you wait to fix your system is another month of stress. Another month of money leaking. Another month of losing ground.

Fear doesn't protect you. Fear costs you. Costs you money. Costs you progress. Costs you peace. Costs you years.

OPPONENT 5: *IGNORANCE*

Fifth opponent is invisible.

Ignorance is what you don't know you don't know.

You can't see it. Can't fight it directly. Can't even recognize when it's attacking you because you don't know it's there.

Ignorance is the chasm between what you think you understand about money and what you actually understand. It's the financial principles nobody taught you. The strategies you never learned. The mistakes you don't realize you're making.

Ignorance is also the most dangerous opponent: it doesn't feel like an enemy. It feels like normal. It feels like "this is just how life is."

Living paycheck to paycheck on a six—figure income? That's *Ignorance* telling you it's normal.

Carrying credit card debt at 24% interest while keeping money in a savings account at 0.5%? That's *Ignorance.*

Not knowing how much you actually spend each month? *Ignorance.*

Thinking you can't save because there's nothing left? *Ignorance.*

For providers specifically, *Ignorance* is insidious because you're highly educated. You're smart. You make complex decisions professionally. So you assume you should know this stuff. And when you don't, you feel shame instead of recognizing that financial literacy isn't taught in medical school or nursing programs or anywhere else.

Recognizing this isn't weakness. It's the first sign of someone who is actually ready to learn — and learning is exactly what you're doing right now.

Nobody taught you this. That's not your fault. But staying ignorant after you know you're ignorant? That's a choice. And this book just ended your excuse.

THE RING YOU'RE STANDING IN

These five opponents — *Desire, Distraction, Comparison, Fear, Ignorance* — they don't attack one at a time.

They move as a gang, encircling and jabbing in at you from all directions and from different angles.

Desire makes you want the lifestyle. *Comparison* shows you others have it. *Distraction* overwhelms you with options. *Fear* paralyzes you from making changes. *Ignorance* keeps you from knowing what changes to make.

And the whole time, the stress builds. The weight increases. Your nervous system stays activated—your body's alarm system stuck in the 'on' position. Your cortisol stays elevated—the stress hormone that keeps you wired and tired at the same time. Your sleep gets worse. Your health deteriorates.

That's what financial stress does to the human body. And it's doing it to you right now.

The good news?

You don't have to fight all five opponents at once.

You don't have to defeat them completely.

You just have to build a system that neutralizes them. A system that holds money despite *Desire*. That stays simple despite *Distraction*. That ignores *Comparison*. That moves despite *Fear*. That learns despite *Ignorance*.

That system exists. It's not complicated. It doesn't require perfection.

It requires three things: what you do this minute, what you do this week, and what you do this month.

But before we get to the system itself, I need to show you why the timeline matters. Why "*This Minute, This Week, This Month*" isn't just a catchy phrase. It's the mechanism that makes it all work.

WHAT YOU ACTUALLY NEED

Think of your financial trajectory like aiming a handgun at a target. A millimeter to the left or to the right and a 7 yard shot isn't hitting center. At 15 yards you are on the edge of the target. At 20 yards the instructor will ask you what you are looking at, your target or your neighbors. Imagine where that shot would land at 50 yards?

If you don't understand guns, here's another way to think about it: small mistakes early become huge mistakes later. Like being one degree off course on a plane— that one degree adds up over distance, left uncorrected and you end up hundreds of miles from your intended destination.

Marksman and pilots both make many small corrections over and over to ensure they are ultimately successful in their work. Calculating for precision and accuracy are what they train diligently for.

In either case it is the same. You are looking at where you want to go, but somehow you are way off the desired course. How are you failing? Small actions on a far out enough timeline make for drastic course changes and markedly different results.

So, you don't need $50,000 to solve today's problems.

You don't need someone called a financial advisor who charges $200 an hour to tell you things you already know.

You don't need another app on your phone that's supposed to help you budget.

What you need is a system. Small consistent course corrections that will steer you to your goal. A new way of handling money that produces completely different results. A new way of deciding all the small, seemingly insignificant actions.

And the system that actually works isn't complicated. It is the same core military tactic warriors are trained to use in the heat.

The system is this. And I want you to listen carefully because this is the whole book in one sentence:

See what's happening. Figure out what it means. Choose what to do about it. Do it. Then do it again.

That's it.

No twelve—step programs. No vision boards. No waiting until you "have time to figure it all out."

See what's happening. Figure out what it means. Do something about it. Check how it went. Do the next thing.

Simple. I'm not saying it's *easy*. I'm saying it's simple.

THREE STAGES OF GETTING GOOD AT ANYTHING

In martial arts, we have a concept from Japan. Three stages of getting good at something. It's called shu ha ri. You don't need to remember the Japanese words. But you need to understand what they mean.

Shu—the copying stage. You follow the basic moves exactly as you're taught. You don't improvise. You don't get creative. You don't try to make it your own way. You just repeat the basic movements over and over and over until they're automatic. Until you don't have to think about them anymore.

Ha—the understanding stage. You start to understand why the moves work. You see the principles behind them. You can adapt them to different situations. You understand what you're doing and why it works.

Ri—the mastery stage. You've done it so much, for so long, that you don't even think about the moves anymore. They're just part of you. You just respond naturally. You don't have to think about the forms. You just move.

Getting good with money follows the same path. The same three stages.

Let's put it another way. Here's how you get good at anything—martial arts, basketball, cooking, money, doesn't matter. Same pattern every time.

Three stages. Everyone goes through them. You can't skip stages. You have to walk through them in order.

Stage One: ***Copy***

You follow the basic moves exactly as you're taught.

No improvising. No creativity. No "but what if I did it my way?"

You just repeat the basic movements over and over and over until they're automatic. Until you don't have to think about them anymore.

A kid learning to shoot a basketball: "Bend your knees. Elbow in. Follow through." Over and over. Doesn't matter if it feels weird. Just do it exactly like coach showed you.

Stage Two: ***Understand***

After you've copied the moves enough times, something clicks.

You start to understand why the moves work. You see the principles behind them. You can adapt them to different situations.

Now the kid understands: "Oh, I bend my knees to generate power from my legs. I keep my elbow in so the shot goes straight. I follow through for accuracy." Now he gets it.

Stage Three: ***Master***

You've done it so much, for so long, that you don't even think about the moves anymore. They're just part of you.

You don't think "bend knees, elbow in, follow through." You just shoot. Natural. Automatic. Perfect form without trying.

The kid is now a high school player. Someone throws him the ball. He doesn't think. He just shoots. Swish. That's mastery.

Where You Are Right Now

Right now with money, you're not even at Stage One yet.

You're not copying the basic moves. You're just reacting. Improvising. Hoping something works.

It's like trying to shoot a basketball without anyone ever teaching you how. You're just throwing it at the hoop and hoping. Sometimes it goes in. Mostly it doesn't. You don't know why it works when it works or why it fails when it fails.

This book is going to teach you Stage One. The basic moves. The things that work when you do them consistently, exactly as I show you.

I'm not going to teach you advanced investment strategies. I'm not going to explain complicated financial terms. I'm not going to give you a spreadsheet with forty—seven different categories for your budget.

I'm going to teach you how to see what's happening with your money. How to figure out what it means. How to choose what to do. And how to actually do it. We are going to change how you make your decisions.

Here is the new tool and lens to see all financial decisions, the **SOP:**

1. This minute. Meaning right now. (ie; Cancel gym membership)

2. This week. Meaning over the next seven days. (ie; List and Sell the mountain bike)

3. This month. Meaning over the next thirty days.(ie; Get more work shifts)

This is your new operating system, your new **S**tandard **O**perating **P**rocedure. Everything you do will have three parts to it. No longer will there be a single action. You will be acting, preparing to act again quickly, and planning to act again soon after that. This is the **S.O.P.**; **This minute, This week, This month.**

You'll copy these moves exactly as I show you. You'll repeat them until they're automatic. And then they'll work. Not because they're complicated. Because they're simple and you did them consistently.

That's Stage One. That's where we're going.

After 42 months of doing the basic moves consistently, you'll be at Stage Two. You'll understand why they work. You'll be able to adapt them.

After years of maintaining your footing, you'll hit Stage Three. You won't even think about money anymore. You'll just handle it naturally. Automatically. Perfectly.

But that's later.

Right now, we're learning to shoot the ball. Basic form. Over and over. Until it's automatic.

PROOF the SOP WORKS

Let's consider two different men. Both make the same income. They live in the same city. Same cost of living. Same basic expenses to cover every month.

__**Man number one**__ runs the default system most people run without knowing they're running it. He reacts when money problems hit. He thinks about fixing things. He waits for the right time to make a real plan. He hopes things get better.

Five years later, he's deep in debt. He has no emergency fund—no money saved for when something breaks. He's way behind on saving for when he can't work anymore. And he wakes up at 3 AM doing math in his head that never adds up. He is still thinking about a plan. He is still hoping things get better.

Hope isn't a strategy. Hope is surrender disguised as optimism.

If I could talk to him, I would say, "You're not struggling. You're losing. There's a difference."

Struggling means fighting. Losing means hoping someone else fixes it while your footing deteriorates. Hoping things get better while you do nothing different is just waiting for rescue that isn't coming.

__**Man number two**__ runs the new system I'm going to teach you. He sees what's happening. He figures out what it means. He chooses what to do. He does it. He checks how it went. He does the next thing. Every single week. Doesn't matter if conditions are perfect or not. He just keeps executing the SOP.

Five years later, he has zero debt. He has a solid emergency fund saved. He's putting money away for retirement and it's on track. And he sleeps through the night.

Same income. Same city. Same expenses to cover.

Different system. Completely different life.

You already know this is true because you've seen it happen with raises.

Remember the last time you got a raise at work, or some unexpected extra cash? That moment of relief. "Finally. This will help. Now I can get ahead."

Where did that money go?

Your lifestyle expanded to eat it up. Your expenses grew. The breathing room disappeared. Within a few months, you were right back to where you started.

Why?

Because you didn't have a system to capture that extra money and use it on purpose. Your default operating system—that automatic way you handle money without thinking about it—just absorbed the raise into the chaos.

More money came in. Same chaos came out.

This is why lottery winners go broke. Why athletes lose all they made and more. Why people making six figures still live paycheck to paycheck.

The money doesn't fix the system. You have to fix the system.

THE SEVEN BATTLES

Every man providing for a family faces the same seven battles. You're fighting at least three of them right now. Maybe all seven. And that can be a lot, overwhelming your confidence.

The first battle is the emergency you can't cover. More than half of all providers live without any buffer between normal life and catastrophe. Not major catastrophes. Normal life catastrophes—the things that break, the things that fail, the things that happen to everyone.

Something in your vehicle fails. Something in your dwelling fails. Someone in your family gets hurt. Someone loses work hours. These aren't exceptional events. These are the guaranteed failures of living in physical reality where things break and bodies fail and circumstances change.

But when you have zero buffer, normal failures become existential crises. The mechanical failure doesn't just cost what it costs—it destroys the entire month's position. Creates a cascade where you're recovering for months from one thing that broke. And you feel it. That tightness when anything unexpected happens, because unexpected now means devastating.

This battle isn't new. Every warrior in history who fought without reserves knew this vulnerability. The Roman century that ran out of supplies. The medieval army that lost its supply train. The modern soldier who enters combat with no backup plan. Same principle. Different battlefield. When you fight without reserves, any disruption becomes catastrophic.

The second battle attacks while you're still reeling from the first: the monthly math that doesn't work. Even if no emergency hits this month, you're bleeding. The resources coming in don't match the obligations going out. There's a gap. Sometimes small. Sometimes large. But always there. Always negative. Always requiring you to sacrifice one obligation to meet another.

This is structural failure. The foundation itself doesn't support the load. And no amount of careful management fixes structural problems —you need foundational solutions.

Throughout history, this battle has destroyed more families than any emergency. Not the unexpected crisis. The slow bleeding of a system that doesn't balance. The gradual deterioration of position through a gap that compounds monthly. The death of a thousand cuts where each cut is small but the cumulative damage is fatal.

You've run the calculations a hundred times hoping they'll come out different. They don't. The math doesn't work, and it's not going to work unless something fundamental changes. Not "I need to be more careful this month." Something structural. Something systemic. Because you've already cut what you can cut. You're already being careful. The problem isn't discipline—the problem is the math itself.

And feeding on that gap, growing larger every month you can't close it, comes the third battle: the debt trap. You're making payments. Regular payments. Required payments. And the balances barely move. The debt consumes your payments while barely reducing, like fighting an opponent who absorbs every strike without taking damage.

This is quicksand. The harder you fight using conventional methods, the deeper you sink. Every payment that goes primarily to interest is effort expended without progress gained. And the psychological weight of this battle crushes differently than the others—because you're actively fighting and still losing ground.

The debt attack sequence is designed to extract you from a quagmire the same way you'd get out of it physically—slow, deliberate movement in one direction, not thrashing. Every dollar has one job: to pull you closer to the surface.

The ancient world understood debt slavery. The medieval world understood debt bondage. The modern world calls it different names but the mechanism is identical: You owe labor for past consumption. Your future work is already obligated to past decisions. And until the obligation is cleared, you're fighting with a weight you can't put down.

At current trajectory, making minimum required payments, the debt will outlast your prime working years. You'll pay double or triple what you originally borrowed. And every month the gap forces you to add new debt while trying to eliminate old debt. You're bailing water into a sinking boat while the leak gets bigger.

The fourth battle whispers from the future while the others scream in the present: retirement impossibility. The position you should be securing while fighting present battles gets sacrificed repeatedly on the altar of immediate survival. And the timeline to build stability shrinks faster than position grows.

This battle is invisible until it's too late. The emergency screams for attention today. The gap bleeds you every month. The debt crushes you constantly. But retirement whispers from decades away, easy to ignore, easy to defer, easy to sacrifice.

Until suddenly it's not decades away. It's years away. Then it's too late. And the warrior who won every tactical battle lost the strategic war because he never secured his future position while fighting his present battles.

You check your retirement position maybe once a year because looking more often is too depressing. The number is a fraction of what it should be. Not half. Not a quarter. A fraction so small that projection calculators refuse to give you an end date—they just show an error like the math broke.

You know you should be building this position. You've known for years. But there's always something else. The gap needs closing. The debt needs paying. The emergency needs covering. Retirement is decades away. These problems are right now. So the future gets sacrificed for the present, month after month, year after year, until the runway to build stability is shorter than the time required to build it.

The fifth battle is fragility itself: the one crisis from disaster vulnerability. You're one disruption away from complete collapse. One loss of income. One major failure. One unexpected crisis. Your entire world falls apart not because you did anything wrong but because you never built resilience into your operating system.

Fragility is the starting point—not the ending. Every system in this book exists to move you from fragile to resilient, one piece at a time. You are already in that process.

Every military force understands defensive depth. You don't defend only at the front line. You build layers of defense so that penetration of one layer doesn't mean total collapse. You build redundancy. You build backup systems. You build the capacity to absorb hits and maintain position.

But you're defending only at the front line with no depth, no reserves, no backup. One breakthrough and stability collapses in weeks. The dwelling. The vehicle. Maybe custody if you can't prove stable housing. That's not a defensive position. That's a death trap waiting for the first real attack.

This is the situation you're building out of—not the situation you're stuck in. Creating financial defensive depth means a single breach doesn't collapse the whole structure. The emergency fund is the primary layer. If it gets breached—and it will—the buffer behind it absorbs the impact. The buffer starts small. The depth gets built. That's the whole point of what comes next.

And you know this. You feel it every time there's uncertainty at work. Every time leadership schedules an unexpected meeting. Every time you hear rumors about changes coming. That spike of adrenaline, that tightness in your throat, because you know: one bad conversation and the shaky financial structure you are standing on falls apart.

You can't eliminate every threat. The goal is to mitigate the damage when threats materialize—to make each crisis a contained problem rather than a system-wide failure.

The sixth battle cuts differently than the others because it's about identity, not just resources: the provider inadequacy. You can't provide what you see others providing. Can't give your family what other families have. Can't deliver the opportunities, the experiences, the advantages.

You provide the fundamentals. Shelter. Food. Safety. The baseline. But the extras? The opportunities? The experiences other families seem to access easily? You can't deliver. And every shortfall lands like evidence that you're failing at your primary purpose.

Provider who can't provide. Protector who can't protect adequately. The weight of this battle isn't just practical—it's existential. It attacks who you are, not just what you have.

Every father in history has felt this. The hunter who returned with empty hands. The farmer whose crops failed. The craftsman whose business declined. The worker whose wages couldn't stretch. Different economies. Same inadequacy. Same shame. Same weight of falling short.

You are not alone in this. You never were. The weight feels private, but it is ancient and shared—and men have carried it through and come out the other side.

Your children ask for things. Reasonable things. Things their peers have. And you have to say no. Not because you don't want to provide. Because you can't. The math doesn't work. The position doesn't support it. And every no reinforces the narrative that you're not enough.

And binding all six battles together, making each one harder to fight, comes the seventh battle: the silent isolation. You carry all of this alone. You don't tell anyone because admitting the struggle feels like admitting you failed. Like admitting you're not the provider you're supposed to be. Like admitting you can't handle it.

So you carry it. In silence. The weight getting heavier every month. And the isolation makes every other battle harder because you're fighting without support, without perspective, without accountability, without the backup every warrior needs.

But the isolation compounds every other battle. The emergency hits harder when you face it alone. The gap widens faster when nobody knows it exists. The debt grows heavier when you carry the shame privately. The retirement crisis deepens when you have no one pushing you to act. The fragility intensifies when you have no support structure. The inadequacy crushes more when you compare your private struggle to everyone else's public success.

This is the part that changes when you let one person in. Just one. The weight doesn't vanish, but it becomes something two people carry instead of one. That is already different.

And all of it—every single battle—gets harder in isolation than it would be with one person who knows the truth and holds you accountable.

This minute. One action you can take in the next ten minutes or less.

This week. Seven days. Three to seven specific things you can do.

This month. Thirty days. A systemic change—a change to your underlying system that sticks—you can make.

Not someday when you have time. Not when conditions are perfect. This minute. This week. This month.

THE PYRAMID YOU'VE BEEN STANDING ON

In 1943, an American psychologist named Abraham Maslow published a paper that changed how we understand human motivation. He wasn't writing about money. He was writing about human needs—and the order in which they must be met.

His insight was deceptively simple: needs have a sequence. You cannot reliably pursue higher needs until lower needs are secured. Not because you're weak or undisciplined. Because that's how human psychology is built.

He drew it as a pyramid.

At the base: survival. Food. Shelter. Physical safety. The biological necessities. Until these are covered, the brain will not—cannot—focus on anything else. It is in threat response. Filtered through one question: *am I safe right now?*

One level up: security. Stability. Predictability. The ability to anticipate tomorrow with some confidence. Income that covers obligations. A buffer against the unexpected. When this level is missing, the brain stays in a low-grade emergency state even when no immediate threat exists. That's the 3 AM math. That's the constant background hum of dread. It isn't anxiety disorder. It's your brain accurately reporting that your security layer is compromised.

One level up from that: belonging. Connection. The relationships that make the fight worth fighting. The people who know what you're carrying. When survival and security are threatened, connection gets sacrificed first. You go quiet. You protect the secret. You fight alone because admitting the struggle feels like failure. You lose the belonging layer to protect what little security you have left.

Above that: esteem. The ability to see yourself as capable, competent, worthy of respect—including your own. The provider who can't provide. The man who should be building and isn't. This battle doesn't just cost money. It costs how you see yourself. And you can't fight that battle well when the three layers beneath it are compromised.

At the top of the pyramid, Maslow placed self-actualization—the full expression of who you can become. The version of yourself who operates from strength instead of fear. Who engages with the future as opportunity rather than threat.

That version of you exists. He's not a fantasy. He's what happens when the layers beneath him are finally built.

Look at the seven battles again through this lens.

The emergency you can't cover—that's the base of the pyramid. Survival threatened by the things that break. When you have no buffer, your brain is running survival calculations constantly. That's not a money problem. That's a threat response that won't turn off until the base layer is secured.

The monthly math that doesn't work and the debt trap—that's the security layer compromised. The gap and the debt together create the low-grade emergency state. The feeling that no matter what you do, you're falling behind. Your brain is not broken. It is correctly identifying that your security layer is missing.

The retirement impossibility and the one-crisis-from-disaster fragility—still the security layer, but extended. Short-term security and long-term security are both gone. The brain cannot plan well across decades when it cannot trust next month.

The provider inadequacy—that's esteem. The identity wound. The battle that attacks not what you have but who you are. And notice: it cannot be healed at the esteem level. You cannot think your way to feeling adequate while survival and security are compromised beneath it. The shame doesn't lift until the layers it's standing on get built.

The silent isolation—that's belonging. The connection that gets sacrificed to protect the secret. The weight that doubles when carried alone and halves when shared. You can't access the belonging layer fully while fighting for the layers beneath it.

This is why the battles feel impossible to solve simultaneously. You're not failing to multitask. You're trying to build the top of a pyramid while the foundation is missing. The human mind under genuine threat narrows its focus to the threat. Long-term planning becomes cognitively inaccessible when the base isn't secure. You literally cannot think well about retirement while your brain is running emergency calculations about this month.

Maslow didn't design this to limit you. He mapped it so you could work with it instead of against it.

The campaign in this book follows the pyramid structure. It's what we are using as a blueprint. You build the base first. Then the next layer. Then the next. In sequence. Each layer unlocking the capacity to build the new one above it.

The emergency fund is the base of the pyramid secured. The moment that buffer exists, something shifts—not just in the account balance but in how your brain processes tomorrow. The threat response quiets. The narrowed focus opens slightly.

Close the gap and the security layer stabilizes. Clear the debt and it solidifies. Build the retirement account and the long-term version of security clicks into place. Now esteem has something to stand on. Now connection can be rebuilt without the weight of shame beneath it.

The 42 months isn't arbitrary. It's the time it takes to build the pyramid—one layer at a time, in the order that human psychology requires.

You haven't been failing to climb. You've been trying to start from the wrong level.

Start at the base. That's where the whole structure begins.

YOU NEED A SYSTEM

The difference between the two men in this chapter isn't income or luck or circumstance. It's whether they have a system. One of them does. The other is hoping conditions improve on their own.

You just picked up a system—a step-by-step set of moves for exactly the situation you're in. The clock starts when you decide it starts. It doesn't require a Monday. It doesn't require a clean slate or a better month. It requires one move, followed by another.

The next chapter names the thing that's been stopping you. Once you can see it, you can fight it.

CHAPTER 2
NAME THE ENEMY

"The greatest victory is that which requires no battle." - Sun Tzu

Name your most valuable asset. Right now. Go. > You took too long. You just bled out ten seconds of the only resource you can't reinforce, resupply, or recover. Your damn time.

If you still have some, there's hope. But let's be clear: I don't want you seeking my counsel when you're old, gray, and defeated. If you spent your life eating croissants on a beach, fine—at least you enjoyed the extraction. But if you killed yourself working and you're standing there old and broke with nothing but a stressed-out body to show for it? You did it wrong. You traded your life for a bad deal, and there are no do-overs. Time flows in one direction, and yours is trickling away.

Look at it this way: You trade your time for currency. It is a literal energy exchange. Money is simply stored energy, held in reserve until you decide where to deploy it—a house, a mission, a retirement. Since time is your primary asset, the number one enemy is anything that usurps that energy. What is draining your clock? What is preventing your best application of your currency?

It's the time wasted frozen in fear and ignorance, facing a decision without a course of action.

It's 0300.

You're awake. Again.

Your spouse is asleep next to you, or maybe you're on the couch in a quiet apartment. It doesn't matter. You are currently "In the Box." You are running the same calculations you've run a hundred times before, like a computer program stuck in a recursive loop.

...if I cut the streaming services... if I skip lunch... if I negotiate the bill...

Round and round. The same math. The same math that failed you yesterday. Sadly, you're not solving the problem. You're just **calculating the defeat.**

You know what needs to happen. You've known for months. You need to cut expenses, call the creditors, and find more revenue. You need to **Engage.** But you're lying there, frozen.

Why? Because the real enemy isn't the $450 shortfall. The $450 is just the terrain.

The real enemy is paralysis, the quintessential mental "Vapor Lock." In the tactical world, Vapor Lock happens when a man is hit with more data than his brain can process without a system. When you don't have a **Trouble Tree Diagnostic**—a pre-set list of "If This, Then That"—your brain defaults to the "Spinning Wheel of Death." You aren't inactive because you're lazy; you're inactive because you're waiting for a "Perfect Move" that doesn't exist.

Frozen is a temporary state, but it's a deadly one. In a gunfight, if you stay frozen, you die. In finance, if you stay frozen, time and revenue is lost while the interest eats you alive.

The SOP breaks the freeze. It doesn't make the math easier; it provides the "Tap Root"—the one central truth you can grab onto when the wind starts blowing. It replaces the "What if?" with your **Standard Operating Procedure (SOP).** What to do **this minute** – action now, move, get clear, and get a plan together. **This week,** enact another facet of your planned response. **This month,** commit multiple actions towards completing your plan.

But there is one critical piece of kit missing. We need to feed an intelligent plan into our SOP. What to do "this minute", what to do, "next week.", and how to plan for "next month".

Data.

We need the recon, a financial status report, and an accurate sight picture of the landscape. We need quality information, we need to process it efficiently, accurately and then we need to act on it. Then we need to do that again, quicker.

So what is the process that feeds our **SOP?**

OODA: THE DECISION CYCLE

In the 1950's, a fighter pilot named Colonel John Boyd was studying why some pilots won dogfights and others didn't.

He noticed something. The pilot who won wasn't always the one with the faster plane or the bigger guns. The winner was the pilot who could complete their decision cycle faster.

Boyd called it the OODA loop. Four steps every decision goes through:

Observe. See what's happening. Enemy plane at two o'clock. Altitude changing. Speed increasing.

Orient. Figure out what it means. He's setting up an attack run. He's got advantage on me right now.

Decide. Choose your response. I need to dive left and come up behind him.

Act. Do it. Employ the maneuver.

Then you observe the result. Did it work? What's he doing now? And you run the loop again.

The pilot who completes that cycle faster wins. Not because his plane is better. Because his decision—making is faster.

Observe. Orient. Decide. Act. Loop back to observe. Repeat.

Speed of the cycle determines who wins.

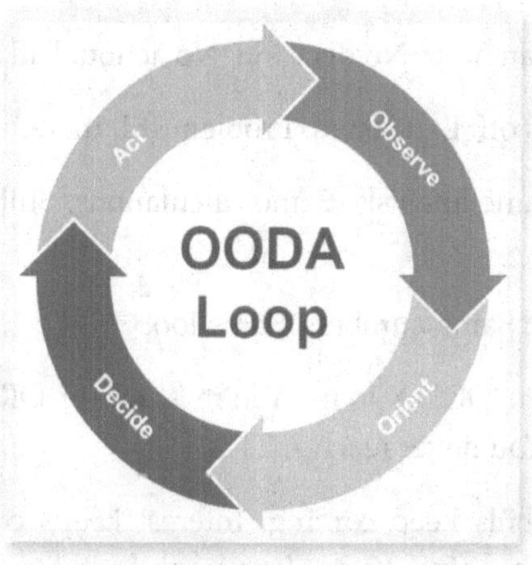

What Boyd discovered changed military strategy forever: You don't need perfect information to start the cycle. You need to start the cycle, get feedback, and adjust. Let that sink in. It means action beats inaction, even with limited info.

The pilot who waits for perfect information before acting is the pilot who gets shot down. Because while he's gathering information, the other pilot has already acted, observed the result, and acted again.

Faster loops beat perfect information.

Your financial situation operates the same way.

You're in a fight. Not with your credit card company. Not with your boss who won't give you a raise. You're in a fight with time and circumstances that keep changing.

The winner is whoever can run faster decision cycles.

Let's apply a broken OODA loop to handling money:

0300 Tuesday. You wake up. Run the numbers in your head.

OBSERVE: You're $450 short this month.

ORIENT: "Could work extra hours... but when? Could cut expenses... but which ones? Could ask for paycheck advance... but that makes next month worse. Could..."

You lie there for an hour. No decision. No action. Fall back asleep.

0600: Alarm goes off. Exhausted. Problem still there.

1900 Tuesday: Same analysis. Same calculations. Still no decision. Still no action.

0300 Wednesday: Same numbers. Same loop.

That's the broken OODA loop. You're stuck in ORIENT. You never reach DECIDE. You never reach ACT.

Meanwhile the bills keep coming. Interest keeps compounding. The situation keeps changing. You're frozen while reality keeps moving.

SEVEN PARALYSIS PATTERNS

Paralysis doesn't look the same for everyone. It shows up in different patterns, and you're stuck in at least one of these right now. Maybe three or four of them simultaneously. Seven specific patterns that keep men frozen, unable to move, running calculations instead of executing solutions.

First pattern: The Overwhelm Cascade. You don't have one problem. You have twelve. Maybe more.

Credit maxed. Rent due. Vehicle failing. Child needs supplies. Phone service overdue. Work hours reduced. Emergency reserve at zero.

Retirement account empty. Insurance deductible too high to use. Dental work needed but unaffordable. The list continues.

Twelve problems hitting simultaneously. Your brain attempts to solve all twelve at once. Process them all. Address them all. Fix them all.

Result? You solve none of them.

This is how the cascade works: You start thinking about the credit situation. Your brain immediately jumps to the rent due next week. Before you can complete one thought about rent, your mind shifts to the vehicle making that noise. Then to the child's upcoming school expenses. Then back to credit. Then to reduced work hours and how that affects the rest of the chain.

You're not thinking through any single problem completely. You're skimming across all twelve problems in rapid succession, never landing long enough to orient, decide, and act on any one of them.

The overwhelm cascade doesn't just make thinking difficult. It makes thinking impossible. Your brain enters a state where it's processing everything and completing nothing. Like trying to hold twelve conversations simultaneously—you're not really in any of them.

Every problem feels equally urgent. Every problem screams for immediate attention. Every problem seems like it should be addressed first. So your brain tries to address them all first, which means it addresses none of them.

This pattern breaks your OODA loop at the most fundamental level. You're trying to observe twelve situations, orient to twelve different meanings, decide on twelve different courses of action, and act on twelve different plans. The human brain cannot process decision cycles at that volume simultaneously.

Throughout history, military commanders understood this principle. When attacked from multiple directions simultaneously, the untrained force panics. They try to defend every position at once. They spread their forces thin across every threatened point. And they lose everywhere because they're strong nowhere.

The trained force does something different. They prioritize. They identify the most critical threat. They mass their forces at that single point. They eliminate that threat completely. Then they turn to the next one.

One threat at a time. Complete elimination. Then move to the next.

The overwhelm cascade keeps you trying to fight all twelve battles at once. You're spreading your mental and emotional resources across all twelve problems, which means you have insufficient resources to actually solve any of them.

And here's what makes the cascade particularly brutal: It compounds itself. The longer you stay in overwhelm, the more problems accumulate. The late payment creates a new problem. The ignored maintenance issue becomes a catastrophic failure. The delayed decision creates consequences that become their own problems.

Twelve problems become fifteen. Fifteen become eighteen. The cascade accelerates until you're completely buried under an avalanche of simultaneous crises, all demanding attention, none receiving adequate response.

The first move out of the overwhelm cascade is to acknowledge the full situation—not to solve it, not to prioritize it yet, just to put it all on the table where you can see it.

Second pattern: The Perfection Trap. You're not going to make a move until you have the perfect plan. The complete understanding. The guaranteed outcome.

You need all the data and details first. Every option researched. Every scenario mapped. Every variable accounted for. Every step plotted from current position all the way to complete financial freedom. You need certainty that the plan will work before you'll engage in the first action.

So you research. You read articles explaining debt elimination strategies. You watch videos about budgeting systems. You study investment approaches. You compare methodologies. You make spreadsheets tracking possibilities. You build comprehensive plans that account for multiple scenarios.

But you never act. This is a loop of never ending polishing of the plan.

Because the plan is never complete enough. There's always one more article to read. One more strategy to understand. One more scenario to account for. One more variable you haven't fully considered. One more potential outcome you haven't planned for.

The perfection trap keeps you in permanent research and planning mode. You're gathering information instead of using information. You're building plans instead of executing plans. You're preparing to act instead of acting.

And while you prepare, the situation deteriorates. The interest compounds. The gap widens. The debt grows. The time available shortens. All while you're still researching the perfect approach.

Striving for 'Perfection' is particularly insidious because it feels productive. Research feels like progress. Planning feels like movement. Understanding feels like improvement. Your brain rewards you with small hits of accomplishment—"I learned something new today"—without requiring you to take any tangible risk.

The perfectionist thinks they're being responsible. Being thorough. Being smart. They're not rushing into anything. They're making sure they get it right.

The deepest deception of the perfection trap is that it masquerades as wisdom. The perfectionist tells themselves they're being careful, thoughtful, responsible. They're avoiding the mistakes that come from rushing into things unprepared.

The perfectionist is avoiding the risk of imperfect action. But they're accepting the certainty of continued deterioration. They're choosing guaranteed slow failure over the risk of imperfect forward movement.

Third pattern: Wrong—Move Paralysis. You're terrified of making the situation worse than it already is.

Right now, things are bad. You know exactly how bad. You've adapted to this specific level of bad. You've developed coping mechanisms for this particular configuration of problems. You know how to survive this exact situation because you've been surviving it for months or years.

But if you make a move—any move—and it's the wrong move, you might make things worse. And worse than the current bad might push you past your capacity to cope. Worse might be the thing that finally breaks you. Worse might be unbearable.

So you don't move. Better to stay in familiar suffering than risk unfamiliar disaster.

This pattern shows up in specific ways: You won't call creditors to negotiate lower payments because "what if they close my account entirely?" You won't cut certain expenses because "what if I cut something important and regret it later?" You won't take additional work because "what if the extra income isn't worth the time and I just exhaust myself for nothing?"

What if. What if. What if.

Your brain generates catastrophic outcomes for every possible action. Not realistic risk assessment. Catastrophic thinking. The worst possible version of every scenario treated as the most likely outcome.

You imagine calling the credit card company. They don't just refuse your negotiation request—they accelerate your payment schedule, raise your interest rate, and report you as high—risk. The call that was supposed to help makes things worse. So you don't call.

This is the deepest trap of wrong—move paralysis: It makes inaction feel responsible. Feel prudent. Feel like the smart play. You're not frozen out of fear—you're making the wise choice to avoid unnecessary risk. You're being careful. You're protecting what little stability you have left.

But inaction isn't neutral. Inaction is still a choice, and that choice has consequences. Guaranteed consequences. While you're avoiding the hypothetical risk of making it worse through action, you're accepting the certainty of making it worse through inaction.

The debt compounds. The gap widens. The timeline shortens. The fragility intensifies. All guaranteed outcomes of inaction. All happening right now while you're protecting yourself from the imaginary disasters that might result from taking action.

Warriors throughout history understood that freezing in combat is the most dangerous position. The soldier who freezes trying to decide the perfect move gets shot. The fighter who hesitates evaluating which technique to use gets hit. Movement—even imperfect movement—is superior to optimal stillness.

Because the enemy doesn't freeze. The enemy keeps attacking. In your case, the enemy is time and compound interest and accumulated consequences. They don't pause while you deliberate. They keep advancing while you stay frozen.

But here's what else doesn't freeze: your capacity to act. Even now. Even in this position. The next move exists and you can take it.

And the longer you stay frozen, the worse the situation becomes, which makes the potential consequences of action feel even more catastrophic, which deepens the paralysis. The pattern feeds itself. Each day of inaction makes action feel more dangerous. Each week of paralysis makes movement feel more risky.

Fourth pattern: Path Invisibility. You can see where you are. You can see where you need to be. But the path between those two points is completely invisible.

You know your current position: Significant debt. Negative monthly gap. Zero buffer. No retirement savings. One crisis from complete collapse.

You know the required destination: Zero debt. Positive monthly margin. Substantial buffer. Growing retirement account. Resilient position.

The distance between those two points feels infinite. The gap seems impossible to cross. When you try to imagine the path from here to there, you see nothing. Just an enormous chasm with no bridge, no rope, no way across.

So you don't start walking. Because you can't see where to walk. The path is invisible, therefore the destination is unreachable, therefore attempting the journey is pointless.

This is an orientation problem. You're orienting to the entire distance between current state and desired state as a single overwhelming gap. Your brain tries to process the complete journey all at once. Tries to see every step simultaneously. Tries to map the entire route before taking the initial step.

Can't be done. The human mind cannot see the complete path to distant goals from the starting position. The view from here doesn't extend that far. The terrain in between isn't visible from ground level.

But here's what you're missing: You don't need to see the entire path. You only need to see the next step.

Every journey in human history worked this way. The explorer didn't see the complete route across an unknown continent before starting. They saw the next day's travel. They walked that day. Then they saw the next day's route. They walked that. Step by step. Day by day. Until they crossed the continent.

Path invisibility keeps you frozen at the starting point, staring at the distant destination, demanding to see the entire route mapped in detail before you'll take one step. And because the entire route isn't visible from the starting point, you never take that first step. You stay frozen. Staring. Waiting for a complete map that will never appear.

The whole route doesn't need to be visible. Just the next step. And the next step is always clearly defined in this system. That's its entire purpose.

That's how distant destinations get reached. Not through complete route visibility before starting. Through taking the visible next step, then the next, then the next, until you're standing at the destination you couldn't see the path to from the beginning.

Fifth pattern: Decision Fatigue. Every single day you make dozens of financial micro—decisions. Each one small. Each one seemingly insignificant. All of them depleting your limited decision—making capacity.

Coffee at home or purchased at a shop. Lunch packed or bought. Name brand or store brand. Fix the broken item or live with it broken. Pay this bill now or defer it to cover that bill. Drive or walk. Heat higher or put on layers. Each individual decision feels minor. Collectively, they drain you.

Your brain has a daily budget for decisions. A limited capacity. Your mind has a finite ability to process quickly and accurately.

And your financial situation requires constant small decisions. Morning to night. Dozens per day. Each one requiring you to evaluate options, consider consequences, make the necessary choice.

By the time evening arrives—the time when you should be making the big strategic decisions that would actually change your trajectory—your decision making capacity is completely depleted. You've spent it all on survival level, micro decisions throughout the day.

The big decisions require the most capacity. "Should I restructure my entire approach to money?" "Should I complete a systematic debt elimination plan?" "Should I commit to forty—two months of disciplined performance?" These are heavy decisions. Complex decisions. They require significant mental resources to process properly.

Sometimes you need a calm moment to come up with a unique solution that requires your artistic flair to imagine. You need space and energy for your artistic side to appear.

So the strategic decisions don't happen. They get deferred. "I'll think about this tomorrow when I'm fresh." Tomorrow comes. Same pattern. Same depletion. Same deferral. The strategic decisions never receive adequate decision—making capacity because the capacity gets consumed by tactical survival before strategy ever gets considered.

The lack of strategic decisions means your tactical situation never improves. The unchanged tactical situation continues requiring constant micro—decisions. The constant micro—decisions continue depleting capacity before strategy gets addressed. Round and round. Strategic paralysis maintained by tactical exhaustion.

Throughout human history, effective leaders understood decision fatigue. They automated as many small decisions as possible to preserve capacity for large decisions. They wore the same clothing daily. They ate the same meals. They followed the same routines. Because they understood that preserving decision making capacity for critical choices required eliminating unnecessary choices elsewhere.

Einstein's identical suits. Military uniforms. Monastic routines. Presidential schedules automated down to the minute. All serving the same purpose: Reduce trivial decisions to preserve capacity for significant decisions.

Your OODA loop runs perfectly well on small tactical decisions. Observe lunch options. Orient to cost and nutrition. Decide on most economical choice. Act by selecting that option. Loop complete. Repeat for next small decision.

But the strategic loop—observe entire financial system, orient to systemic problems, decide on major structural changes, act on complete restructuring—that loop requires substantial capacity. Capacity you don't have because it's already been consumed by tactical loops.

The pattern keeps you functioning tactically while failing strategically. You're making dozens of small decisions adequately while never making the large decisions that would eliminate the need for so many small decisions.

Sixth pattern: Shame Silence. You cannot talk about this situation with anyone. Not your spouse. Not your family. Not your friends. No one.

Because talking about it requires admitting you're struggling. Admitting you can't handle the responsibility you're supposed to handle. Admitting you're failing at the one thing you're supposed to succeed at. Admitting you're not the provider you're supposed to be.

The admission feels impossible. So you keep silent. You carry it alone. You maintain the appearance that you've got it all under control, it's manageable, meanwhile internally you're drowning.

It feels impossible until it doesn't. Most people who've said those words describe a relief on the other side they didn't expect. The impossible thing becomes the turning point.

Your wife asks, "How we are doing financially?", You say fine. She asks if you are doing okay. You say yes. She senses something's wrong. You deflect. Change the subject. Build distance. Protect the secret.

Because the secret feels safer than the truth. The isolation feels more bearable than the shame of admission.

The secret costs more than the truth. Every day of silence is another day of carrying alone what was meant to be carried together.

And maybe you are right not to stress her too. She has enough to deal with and worrying her to would just make both of you miserable.

But carrying it alone means you have no external input. No alternative perspectives. No reality checks on your thinking. No one to tell you when you're catastrophizing. No one to point out the obvious solution you're missing. No one to push you when you need pushing. No one to hold you accountable when you're reverting.

Shame silence keeps you isolated. And isolation compounds every other paralysis pattern.

The silence ends the moment you decide it does. Not when the numbers look better. Not when you've fixed something first. Right now, exactly as things are.

The overwhelm cascade gets worse when you're processing twelve problems alone with no one to help you prioritize.

The perfection trap tightens when you have no one to tell you "good enough is better than perfect plan that never executes."

Wrong—move paralysis intensifies when you have no one to reality—check whether the catastrophic outcomes you're imagining are actually realistic.

Path invisibility persists when you have no one who's walked the path to tell you "the next step is visible, just take it."

Decision fatigue crushes harder when you're making every decision alone with no one to share the load.

Identity threat remains unaddressed when you have no one to tell you "struggling doesn't mean failing, fighting through it means succeeding."

Every pattern worse in isolation. Every pattern easier to break with support.

But shame prevents you from accessing support. Shame tells you that admitting the struggle means admitting you're inadequate. That asking for help means proving you're weak. That revealing the truth means destroying the identity you've built.

What shame calls weakness, courage calls honesty. The two look identical from the outside—someone deciding to speak the truth about where they are.

So you stay silent. You carry it alone. You run your OODA loops inside your own head with no external perspective to correct your errors.

Your observations might be wrong. You might be seeing the situation more catastrophically than it actually is. But with no external input, you'll never know.

Your orientation might be skewed. You might be interpreting what the situation means through distorted lens. But with no alternative perspective, you can't recognize the distortion.

Your decisions might be terrible. You might be choosing the worst possible actions based on flawed observation and skewed orientation.

But with no one checking your logic, you'll employ bad decisions with full confidence.

Eight words end it: 'I need help. Here's what's actually happening.' Eight words and you are no longer alone in this fight.

Throughout history, warriors understood that fighting alone is how you die. Every military force operates in units. Every successful fighter trains with partners. Every effective force has communication, coordination, mutual support.

The lone warrior is mythology. Entertainment. Fiction. In reality, the fighter who insists on operating alone gets destroyed by the coordinated force that operates together.

You are reading a book written by someone who found a way through. That means a way through exists—one that doesn't require you to be stronger than you are right now.

Seventh pattern, and the deepest: Identity Threat. This is the one that's hardest to admit because it operates below conscious awareness. It's the pattern that drives the other patterns without you recognizing it's happening.

You are a provider. That's not just what you do. That's who you are. Your identity. Your purpose. Your fundamental definition of self.

Provider means you handle financial responsibility. You make sure the family is housed, fed, secure. You manage money competently. You build stability. You create safety. You fulfill the fundamental duty.

Admitting financial struggle cuts at identity—at the part of you built around being the provider, the one who handles things. Acknowledging the gap is the principle act of fulfilling that duty.

That's not just admitting a problem exists. That's admitting you might be failing at being who you're supposed to be. That's threatening the foundation of your identity itself.

And your brain will do almost anything to protect you from that threat. It will distort observation. It will skew orientation. It will paralyze decision—making. It will maintain harmful patterns. Anything to avoid the psychological devastation of complete identity collapse.

So your brain protects you through selective observation. It minimizes the severity. It finds evidence that things aren't as bad as they seem. It compares your situation to worse situations and finds comfort in not being at the bottom. It generates explanations for why the struggle isn't really your fault—economic conditions, unexpected circumstances, systemic issues beyond your control.

All of it serving one purpose: Protecting your provider identity from the threat of acknowledging that you're not providing adequately.

But this protection mechanism is actually destruction mechanism. By preventing you from observing the situation accurately, your brain prevents you from responding to the situation effectively. By protecting you from the psychological pain of acknowledging provider inadequacy, your brain maintains the practical reality of inadequacy. Your brain is working against your best interest. A case of you, being your own worst enemy.

You can't fix what you won't acknowledge. Can't address what you won't see. Can't solve what you're in denial about.

This pattern is why men can be drowning while insisting they're fine. Why they can be months from complete collapse while, from the outside looking in, the facade of control is projected. Why they can be carrying crushing weight while presenting composed exterior.

The identity threat is so severe that admitting the struggle feels more dangerous than continuing the struggle. Acknowledging provider inadequacy feels more devastating than living in provider inadequacy.

So they choose the lie that protects identity over the truth that threatens it. They choose comfortable denial over uncomfortable acknowledgment. They choose identity preservation over practical improvement.

And they stay stuck. For years. Sometimes decades. Sometimes until complete collapse forces acknowledgment that can no longer be denied.

Throughout history, the most dangerous enemy has always been self—deception. The army that believes it's winning while it's losing makes catastrophic strategic errors. The fighter who believes he's dominating while he's being dominated gets knocked out by the punch he didn't see coming. The leader who believes his position is secure while it crumbles takes no defensive action until it's too late.

Self—deception is more dangerous than external threat because you can't fight what you can't see. And you can't see what your identity depends on not seeing.

Identity threat keeps you in self—deception. Keeps you observing selectively. Keeps you orienting to a distorted version of reality. Keeps you making decisions based on fantasy rather than fact.

And the only way to break this pattern is to redefine what "provider" means. To separate the identity from the current financial state. To recognize that providing is about character, not current position. That the willingness to face truth and fight through difficulty is what makes you a provider, not the absence of struggle.

The man drowning in debt who refuses to acknowledge it is not providing. The man drowning in debt who acknowledges it honestly and fights through it consistently is providing. Same financial position. Completely different provider status.

Character defines provider identity. The willingness to face reality, make hard choices, utilize discipline, fight through difficulty, and model strength for those who depend on you.

That's what provider means. And struggle doesn't threaten that identity. Denial threatens that identity. Giving up threatens that identity. Hiding threatens that identity.

But fighting? Fighting through honest acknowledgment and consistent action? That fulfills provider identity even while the financial position is broken.

These seven patterns don't operate in isolation. They compound each other. Feed each other. Strengthen each other.

Overwhelm drives perfection seeking. Perfection seeking intensifies wrong—move paralysis. Wrong—move paralysis creates path invisibility. Path invisibility increases decision fatigue. Decision fatigue reinforces shame silence. Shame silence protects identity threat. Identity threat maintains all the other patterns.

You're not stuck in one pattern. You're stuck in a system of interlocking patterns that reinforce each other and maintain paralysis as the stable state.

Breaking one pattern weakens the others. Take action on the visible next step and you break path invisibility. Path invisibility breaking makes wrong—move paralysis less convincing. Wrong—move paralysis reducing makes perfection trap less necessary. Perfection trap releasing makes overwhelm cascade more manageable.

But you have to break one to weaken the others. And you break one through deliberate action despite the pattern screaming at you not to.

That's what the next chapters teach. How to break each ingrained pattern. How to act despite overwhelm. How to move despite paralysis. How to complete OODA loops faster than the patterns can reassert themselves.

OLD AND SCARED — WON'T ENGAGE

The seven patterns above are about not knowing what to do. This one is for the man with thirty years of experience and nothing to show for it. The grizzled veteran whose time down range should have added up to more monetary success.

The problem isn't the change that is coming down the pipe right at you, it's the inability to realize it is already happening. Change presents itself as a flicker of data at first, an opportunity to front run a problem.

You've seen this before. You recognize the pattern. You know exactly what to do. The change is coming — you can feel it, you can see the indicators, you've watched this movie before — and you're standing there doing nothing. Not because you're confused. Because the last time you trusted your read, you moved, and you were wrong. You acted and it cost you. Maybe you were early or late. Maybe you over corrected. Maybe it reversed the moment you committed. Doesn't matter. You moved with confidence and it blew up in your hands.

So you stopped moving, stopped risking, stopped putting yourself on the front lines.

Now you watch the jar of milk tilt toward the edge of the counter. You see it happening. You could catch it. You don't catch it. Because catching it means committing to a read that might be wrong again — and you've decided, somewhere below conscious thought, that you can't afford another wrong read. So you wait. You let it fall. You clean it up.

Broken has known parameters. Cleanup is calculable. And nothing can be traced back to you, because you didn't even move. Luck tipped the milk. Bad luck won. Not your fault.

That's what you tell yourself. A simple accident. Accidents happen right?

Here's what's actually true: you've handed the wheel to luck and called it wisdom. You've dressed up fear as patience. Every day you don't engage, the thing you were afraid of getting wrong gets worse — guaranteed, compounding, with interest. The jar you wouldn't catch has been on the floor for years now. You're still cleaning it up.

This is what it looks like at sixty. A man who saw it coming, knew what to do, and waited until the parameters were undeniable and the best moves were gone. Cautious. Reasonable. Broke.

You need to become confident enough to act instinctively in your best interest as change is happening. You need to get the money decisions right the first time. That's what winning looks like.

EVERY MOVE SERVES THE OBJECTIVE

In a real fight, every movement costs energy.

Good fighters learn something called economy of motion. This means: don't waste energy. Every move should count toward winning." Don't move unless the movement serves winning the fight. Don't duck and weave at every movement from the enemy. Don't move unless a blow is in range and would actually land. Don't waste energy on anything that doesn't help you win.

Bad fighters waste motion constantly. Bouncing around the ring burning energy. Throwing flashy combinations that don't land. Moving for the sake of moving.

They gas out. Run out of energy. Lose.

It's like being in a rocking chair. You've been in that rocking chair with your finances. Lots of motion. Lots of activity. Thinking about budgets. Planning to save. Meaning to tackle debt. Reading articles. Watching videos. Feeling busy.

Zero progress. The rocking chair keeps rocking, staying in place. You keep going nowhere.

Economy of motion applied to money means: every action must serve winning the financial fight. Every dollar must serve securing position. Every hour of work must move you forward.

Stop rocking. Start fighting.

Economy of motion means every step, every punch, every movement is calculated. Does this serve my objective? If yes, do it. If no, don't.

Your money operates the same way.

Every expense is a movement. Movements cost resources. Resources are limited.

Does this expense serve my objective? Objective: get stable. Get out of crisis. build stability.

If the expense serves that objective, make it. If it doesn't, don't make it.

Most people waste motion constantly. Expenses that serve nothing. Subscriptions they don't use. Convenience purchases that don't matter. Lifestyle expenses that don't improve anything.

All of it burns resources that could go toward the objective.

Economy of motion applied to money: Every dollar serves the objective or it doesn't get spent.

Right now, you're wasting motion. Not because you're stupid. Because you're trying to serve too many objectives at once.

Serve the stability objective. Serve the comfort objective. Serve the social expectation objective. Serve the deserve—something—nice objective. Serve the keep—up—with—others objective.

Can't serve five objectives. You serve one objective until it's achieved. Then move to the next.

Right now, your objective is: break paralysis and start moving.

Every thought serves that objective or you dismiss it. Every action serves that objective or you don't take it.

"Should I research the seventeen different debt payoff strategies to find the optimal one?"

Does that serve breaking paralysis? No. That's perfectionism keeping you stuck.

"Should I take one action this minute that moves me forward even slightly?"

Does that serve breaking paralysis? Yes. Do it.

Economy of motion. Every move serves the objective.

TACTICAL OVERRIDE

You know all this now. You understand paralysis. You recognize which pattern you're stuck in. You know you need to run faster OODA loops.

And you're still frozen.

Understanding the problem doesn't automatically break the paralysis. Sometimes you need an override.

Here's what you do when you're completely stuck:

Stop thinking about money. Start moving physically. (Action beats inaction)

Stand up. Right now if you're listening to this. Stand up.

Go do something physical with your hands. Something that has nothing to do with money.

Grab your "honey—do" list, or a chore you've been putting off. Change the broken light bulb in the fridge. Fix something that's been broken, but you keep putting off. Organize one drawer. Clean one thing. Lube a squeaky door hinge. Build something. Take something apart.

Physical movement with your hands. Requires focus. Produces a visible result.

Your brain is stuck in analysis loops. Thinking about thinking about thinking. Paralyzed.

Physical movement breaks that loop. Your brain has to shift from abstract thinking to concrete doing. From planning to executing. From imagining to creating.

You change the light bulb. Task complete. Visible progress. Proof you can start something and finish it.

That proof—even on something tiny that has nothing to do with money—breaks the mental paralysis.

Scientists discovered something called the Zeigarnik Effect. To put it simply: Unfinished tasks take up mental space. Your brain keeps thinking about them, using energy, creating stress. When you complete a task—even a small one—your brain can let it go. The mental space clears. The stress reduces.

When you complete a task—even a small physical one—you close that loop. Your brain releases the cognitive resources it was using to maintain that task. The completed task gets filed away. The mental tension dissolves.

The financial action now feels possible because you just proved to yourself that you can move. You can execute. You can complete something. You demonstrated that completion is achievable. The tactical override isn't about avoiding the problem. It's about breaking analysis paralysis through physical action so you can return to the problem with the ability to move.

That small victory creates momentum. It reminds your executive function that tasks can be finished, loops can be closed, problems can be solved. And that reminder—backed by immediate physical proof—makes the next, harder task feel less impossible.

I am not recommending a distraction. This is breaking the freeze so you can move on what matters. Now write down the major concern you had earlier. Why? Writing tasks down helps externalize unfinished business, reducing cognitive load and anxiety associated with remembering details down to the minutia. Research shows that simply making a plan for task completion can provide similar psychological relief to actually finishing the task, as your brain treats a solid plan as a promise of future completion

SOP: THIS MINUTE

Objective: To terminate the "Vapor Lock" loop and restore operational command within 10 minutes.

Phase 1: Physical Disruption (The Grounding)

- Move the Frame: Do not stay in bed. The bed is now "The Box." Physically get out of bed and move to a "Command Station" (a kitchen table or desk).
- Biological Reset: Drink 8 oz of cold water. Dehydration spikes cortisol, which fuels anxiety.

- The Light Switch: Turn on a light. Darkness allows the imagination to distort the math. Light forces the eyes to focus on reality.

Phase 2: The Data Dump (The Intel Log)

- Analog Capture: Do not use a phone or laptop (blue light will worsen the sleep disruption). Use a pen and paper.
- Write the "Enemy Strength": Write down the exact number that is scaring you. Not "I'm broke," but "$452.18 short for rent."
- The SOP: Write down the three—and *only* three—actions that could theoretically move that number.

Phase 3: The "Go/No-Go" Decision

- Determine Execution Window: Ask: *"Can I execute any of these three actions at 0315?"* * The Answer is No: Make the plan and set them in an actionable timeline. Writing it down on pen and paper will take it off of your mental baggage load.
- The Command: You are officially Off-Watch.

Phase 4: Re-Entry (The Tactical Sleep)

- The "Brain Dump" Folder: Leave the paper on the table. Tell yourself: *"The data is secured. The plan is logged. I will engage at 0800."*
- Box Breathing: Return to bed and use a 4-count box breath (4 seconds in, 4 hold, 4 out, 4 hold). This tells your nervous system the "combat" is over for the night.

SOP: THIS WEEK

Run one OODA loop per day on small financial decisions.

Monday: One small expense from yesterday. Observe what you spent.

Orient to whether it served your objective. Decide if you'll repeat it. Act on that decision.

Tuesday: Different expense. Same process.

Wednesday: Same process. New expense.

Thursday: By now you're getting faster at the loop. Keep going.

Friday: Same loop. Starting to feel automatic yet?

Saturday: Calculate how many complete loops you ran this week. Should be at least five.

Sunday: Rest day. But notice: you've completed five cycles this week. That's five times you didn't freeze. Five times you moved.

Seven days. Five to seven complete OODA loops on small things.

You're not solving your whole financial situation this week. You're training your brain to complete decision cycles instead of getting stuck in them.

SOP: THIS MONTH

Week one: Daily OODA loops on small decisions. Building the pattern.

Week two: Run loops every other day. Three to four loops this week. Slightly bigger decisions now. Not just coffee. Maybe entire grocery trip. Maybe monthly subscription.

Week three: Daily loops again. Bigger decisions. Should I keep this service? Should I ask for more hours? Should I sell this thing I don't use?

Week four: Multiple loops per day. Your brain is getting faster. Observe, orient, decide, act. Observe, orient, decide, act. The pattern is becoming automatic.

By month's end, you've run 28 to 35 complete decision cycles. Your system is learning to move instead of freeze.

That's the whole point. Train your system to run loops faster than problems compound.

Speed wins. Not perfect information. Not flawless planning. Speed.

WHAT'S NEXT

The next chapter is where the real fight initiates—not with a spreadsheet, but with a $500 buffer between you and the next thing that breaks.

CHAPTER 3
EMERGENCY BLINDNESS

"Every battle is won before it's fought" - Sun Tzu

Your check engine light has been on for two weeks.

You know you need to deal with it. You've been meaning to deal with it. But dealing with it costs money you don't have right now. So you keep driving. Hoping it's nothing serious. Hoping it goes away on its own.

It doesn't go away.

Friday afternoon, the car starts making a noise. A grinding noise that wasn't there this morning. By the time you get home, the noise is worse. By Saturday morning, the car won't start at all.

You call mechanics. Get estimates. The repair costs more than you have in your account.

Your checking account balance won't cover it.

Rent is due soon. Before your next paycheck hits.

The math: The repair costs more than what's available right now. Rent is due—that's the priority. Every dollar has to stretch until the paycheck lands. This is exactly why building a buffer changes your ability to maintain your mental frame under pressure.

The emergency just destroyed your month. Maybe your next month too.

But here's the thing: This wasn't actually an emergency.

THE PREDICTABLE SURPRISE

Check engine lights don't appear randomly. They're warnings. Your car is telling you something needs attention now before it becomes catastrophic later.

You ignored the warning for two weeks. The problem got worse. You risked an entire engine. Now it's catastrophic.

That's not an emergency. That's a predictable failure you treated like a random surprise.

Your water heater is fourteen years old. The average water heater lasts ten to twelve years. Yours is living on borrowed time. When it fails—not if, when—you'll call it an emergency.

It's not. It's a scheduled failure you didn't schedule for.

Your tires are bald. You can see the wear. You know they need replacing. You're hoping they last another few months. When one blows out on the highway, you'll call it an emergency.

It's not. It's a predictable event you didn't prepare for.

Your company has been talking about restructuring for six months.

You've heard the rumors. You've seen the signs. When they lay you off, you'll call it an emergency.

It's not. It was telegraphed—signaled ahead of time—for half a year. You just didn't prepare.

Most of what you call emergencies aren't emergencies. They're predictable events you're treating as surprises because you have no system for seeing them coming and no buffer to absorb them when they hit.

That's emergency blindness. The inability to read the signals before the crisis. The inability to prepare for predictable failures. The tendency to treat scheduled maintenance as unexpected disaster.

READING THE FIGHT BEFORE IT STARTS

In combat sports, there's a concept called the prefight read. You study your opponent before you ever step in the ring. You watch their old fights. You see their patterns. You know their tendencies.

When the fight starts, nothing they do surprises you. You've already seen it. You know what's coming. You're prepared.

The fighter who doesn't do the prefight read gets surprised constantly. "I didn't expect him to throw that combination." You should have. He throws it in every fight. You just didn't study the tape.

Your financial life is the same fight. Same principle.

You can read what's coming if you pay attention to the signals.

Your car is twelve years old with 140,000 miles. Something major will break in the next twelve months. Not might break. Will break. That's not a prediction. That's statistics. Cars with that age and mileage have major repairs coming.

You know this. But you're not preparing for it. You're hoping it doesn't happen. Or hoping it happens after you have more money. Or just not thinking about it.

When it breaks, you'll act surprised. But you shouldn't be. The fight was telegraphed. You just weren't reading it.

Your refrigerator is making a weird noise. Started three weeks ago. Gets louder when the compressor kicks on. That's the prefight signal. Compressor is failing. Refrigerators don't heal themselves. The noise will get worse. Then the fridge stops cooling. Then you're buying a new fridge on an emergency agenda with no time to shop for deals.

Signal was there. You didn't read it.

Your work hours got cut from forty to thirty five per week. Management says it's temporary. Your income just dropped $200 monthly. If you don't adjust your spending immediately, you're creating a $200 monthly gap that will compound into crisis.

The signal is crystal clear. Most people don't adjust. They hope hours get restored. They don't. A small gap becomes a major crisis. Surprise.

Prefight read means looking at what's actually happening and acknowledging what it means. Not what you hope it means. What it actually means.

A "Check Engine" light for two weeks means something is wrong and getting worse. Ignoring it doesn't make it better. It makes it catastrophic.

Once you learn to read these signals, you need something in place to absorb them when they hit. That something is $500.

THE $500 THAT CHANGES YOUR FUTURE

You don't need $18,000 in an emergency fund. That's six months of expenses for most people. That's the impressive number. That's what financial advisors tell you to build.

Forget that number. It's not helpful right now. It's so far away it's meaningless.

You need $500. That's it. Five hundred dollars sitting in an account you don't touch unless something breaks.

$500 matters because: It's enough to cover most small emergencies without destroying your month.

Car repair: $340. You have $500 buffer. Repair gets paid. You still have $160 left. Month survives. You rebuild the buffer over the next sixty days.

Without the buffer, that $340 repair destroys the underpinnings of stability. Can't pay rent. Late fees pile up. Stress compounds. The emergency cascades into disaster.

With the buffer, the emergency is absorbed. Inconvenient, not catastrophic.

That's the difference. $500 standing between you and disaster.

You're thinking: "I don't have $500. I can barely cover my bills. How am I supposed to save $500?"

You're not going to save it through discipline and sacrifice alone. You're going to build it through three actions most people never take.

THREE SOURCES

You have three ways to build $500.

Source one: Cut the waste. Not your whole lifestyle. Just the pure waste. The things you're paying for that you don't actually use or need.

Three subscriptions you don't use anymore. One service you signed up for and forgot about. One monthly payment for something that seemed like a good idea months ago but you haven't touched in weeks.

Redirect all of it to the buffer. Don't let lifestyle expand to eat it. Redirect it the minute you cut it.

Source two: Sell the unused. Look around your space. You have things you bought and don't use. Things sitting in closets or storage. Things you meant to use but never did.

That bike you bought and rode twice. Those tools sitting in the garage untouched for years. That camera equipment you upgraded past. That gaming system you don't play anymore. Those collectibles gathering dust. The second TV. The extra furniture.

It's all worth money. Sitting there doing nothing is worth zero. Converting it to cash builds the buffer.

Source three: Generate additional income. One time extra work. Not a second full time job. One time hustles. Temporary gigs. Task based work.

Help someone move. Deep clean an apartment. Organize someone's garage. Run errands for elderly neighbors. Do deliveries for a weekend. List items online for people who don't want to deal with it. Mow yards. Pressure wash driveways. Whatever work you can pick up and accomplish in a few hours that pays immediate cash.

Three sources. Operating simultaneously. All money redirected to the buffer.

Cut waste. Sell unused items. Generate additional income. These three sources working together build your $500 buffer faster than waiting for one perfect solution.

The buffer gets built. Not from massive lifestyle sacrifice. From eliminating waste, converting unused assets to cash, and generating temporary additional income.

EMERGENCY TEST

Not everything that feels like an emergency is actually an emergency. Your brain will try to convince you that every new crisis is of the highest urgency. Every bill needs immediate money right now. It sends the same level of shock hormones through you, despite vast differences in the situational details and the facts about the objective truth.

Before you drain the buffer, run the emergency test. Three questions. All three must be yes for it to qualify.

Question one: Does it need to happen this week?

Your kid wants new shoes. Nice to have. Not emergency. Can wait until payday.

Your kid's shoes have holes and they're walking in the rain getting their feet soaked. That needs to happen this week. Real need.

Question two: Will not handling it create a bigger problem? If you don't address it now, does it compound into something worse and more expensive?

Check engine light. Ignoring it turns a $200 repair into an $800 repair. That's compound problem. Handle it.

Your phone is two years old and working fine but a new model came out. Not handling it creates zero additional problems. Identified as not emergency.

Question three: Is there a cheaper temporary solution? Can you solve the immediate problem with less money while you figure out the permanent solution?

Car won't start. Full repair is $600. But you can get a jump start for free and drive it to work for a week while you figure out how to pay for the repair. Temporary solution exists. Use it.

Water heater died. Replacing it properly costs $1,200. But you can heat water on the stove and take temporary partial showers for a few days while you shop for the best price and schedule installation. Temporary solution exists. Use it.

All three questions yes? It's an emergency. Use the buffer.

Any question is no? It's not an emergency. It's a want or a non—urgent need. Handle it differently.

The emergency test protects your buffer from things that feel urgent but aren't actually urgent.

SOP: THIS MINUTE

Calculate your current buffer.

Not your checking account balance. The real, planned and sequestered emergency fund. Money set aside specifically for emergencies. Money you don't touch unless something breaks.

For most of you reading this, that number is $0.

Write it down: **Current buffer: $0**

Now write the target: **Target buffer: $500**

That's your gap. $500 between where you are and where you need to be.

You just defined the objective. Build $500 buffer. That's the mission.

SOP: THIS WEEK

Monday: Identify three subscriptions or monthly payments you can cut. Don't cancel them yet. Just identify them. Write down the three things and how much you're paying monthly.

Tuesday: Cancel those three subscriptions. All three. Don't wait. Call or go online and cancel. Get confirmation. Calculate the monthly savings. Write it down.

Wednesday: Walk through your space. Apartment, house, room, wherever you live. Identify ten items you own but don't use. Things with resale value. Things someone would buy. Write them down.

Thursday: Pick the three easiest items to sell from that list. List them online. Facebook Marketplace, Craigslist, OfferUp, wherever. List all three today. Set realistic prices. You want them sold fast, not sitting there for months.

Friday: Identify one source of additional income you could run this weekend or next week. One task. One gig. One piece of work. Something that pays cash for a few hours. Write it down.

Saturday: Follow up on your listings. Respond to messages. Arrange pickups. Close the sales. Take the cash and move it immediately to your buffer account—separate savings account or separate envelope. Don't let it sit in checking where it gets absorbed.

Sunday: Calculate your progress. How much did you cut in subscriptions? How much did you make from selling items? Did you line up the additional income opportunity? Add it all up. That's week one progress toward $500.

You should have meaningful money moved toward your buffer in week one. Not huge. But moving. And moving beats frozen.

SOP: THIS MONTH

Week one: run this WEEK. Cut subscriptions. List items. Identify income opportunity.

Week two: Employ the income opportunity you identified. Help someone move. Do the delivery gig. Whatever you lined up. Get paid. Move the money immediately to buffer. Then identify three more items to sell. List them. Sell them. Money to buffer.

Week three: Review your spending from the previous two weeks. Where did money leak? What got spent that didn't serve the objective? Cut two more things. Identify one more income opportunity. do it this week.

Week four: Calculate total buffer built this month. If you realized gains from all three sources, you've made substantial progress. If you hit $500, you have your first milestone. If you're partway there, you proved you can build it. Keep going next month.

By month's end, you have either a complete $500 buffer or you're substantially closer to it. More importantly, you proved to yourself that you can build it. It's not theoretical. You did it.

THE PREDICTIVE POWER

Once you have the buffer, something changes. Not just financially. Psychologically.

You start seeing problems before they become catastrophic. Because you know you have $500 to handle them if they hit.

The check engine light comes on. Before buffer, you ignore it and hope.

After buffer, you schedule the diagnostic. Catch it early. $200 repair instead of $800 emergency.

The water heater is making noise. Before buffer, you wait until it dies completely. After buffer, you start shopping for replacements now while there's time to compare prices. Save $300 by not buying in emergency mode.

You hear rumors about layoffs at work. Before buffer, you deny and hope. After buffer, you start updating your resume and looking at options now instead of scrambling after termination.

The buffer doesn't just absorb emergencies. It gives you the psychological safety to see them coming and prepare instead of denying and hoping.

That's the real value. Not the $500. The ability to think clearly about risk instead of being paralyzed by it.

THE REBUILD DISCIPLINE

Here's where most people fail.

They build the $500 buffer. Emergency hits. Buffer gets drained to $200.

Then they relax. "I handled the emergency. I survived. I'll rebuild it eventually."

They don't rebuild it. The buffer stays at $200. Next emergency hits. $200 isn't enough. Disaster.

The rule: Every time you drain the buffer, you rebuild it immediately. Top priority. Before anything else.

Emergency cost $300. Buffer is now at $200. Next month's objective isn't treating yourself because you handled the emergency. Next month's objective is getting buffer back to $500. Then to $1,000.

The buffer only works if it gets rebuilt after every use. Otherwise you're back to living one emergency away from disaster.

Discipline isn't building it once. Discipline is rebuilding it every time it gets used.

TACTICAL OVERRIDE

You're in week two. You're supposed to be executing the income opportunity and selling more items.

Week two is where most people stall. Overwhelm sets in. The next move feels invisible. That's normal—and that's exactly when the SOP takes over for you.

Stop thinking about what to sell. Start moving physically.

Go to the area where you have stuff stored. Closet. Garage. Storage unit. Spare room. Wherever you keep things you don't use.

Don't think about value. Don't try to calculate what things are worth. Don't get emotional about whether you might need them someday.

Just pull all of it out and put it into a pile. Physically move items from storage into a giant visible pile.

Don't organize the pile. Don't sort it. Just make a physical pile of unused items in the middle of the space.

Then take a photo of the pile with your phone.

Look at the photo. That's money sitting there. Actual money that people will pay you for.

From the pile, pick three items. Not the most valuable items. The three easiest items to sell. The things you know someone would buy immediately.

List those three items right now. Before you put anything back in storage. List them. Price them reasonably. Get them moving.

The physical act of making the pile breaks the analytical paralysis. You can see the value instead of imagining it. The photo makes it real. Three items get listed. Money starts moving to buffer.

Physical action breaks mental freeze. Every time.

WHAT'S NEXT

Your car has been telling you something for two weeks. Most men in your situation already know the feeling—that quiet dread when something makes a noise it didn't make last month, and you have nothing set aside to deal with it. The check engine light isn't the problem. The empty account behind it is.

The buffer doesn't need to be large to change your level of security. Five hundred dollars between you and the next emergency is the difference between a manageable but bad day and a cascading disaster. That's the first concrete target. Not a financial overhaul. One number. Five hundred.

The next chapter explains why even if you start saving tomorrow, the monthly math might still eat it faster than you can build it. Don't worry, we will close that gap next.

CHAPTER 4
MONTHLY NUMBERS FAIL

"Absorb what is useful. Discard what is not. Add what is uniquely your own." - Bruce Lee

It's the 28th of the month. Your checking account shows barely enough to buy groceries. Rent is due in three days.

Your paycheck hits in five days. So close. If rent was due after the paycheck, you'd be fine. But it's due before. And your paycheck doesn't arrive until after.

A few days. You're a few days short.

Late fee if rent isn't paid on time. That late fee pushes the total higher than your incoming paycheck.

This has happened before. Last month you borrowed from family. The month before that you over drafted and paid fees. The month before that you paid the late rent penalty.

Every month, same problem. Sometimes you make it work. Sometimes you don't. But every month is a scramble.

You're thinking: "I just need one month where nothing goes wrong. One month where an emergency doesn't hit. One month where the timing lines up. Then I can get ahead."

That month never comes. Because the problem isn't the emergencies or the timing.

The problem is the math. Your baseline expenses exceed your baseline income. Every month.

That's called a structural gap. The gap isn't temporary. It's built into the structure. And no amount of hoping for a clean month will fix structural problems.

THE GAP

Let's run the numbers. The math you've been avoiding. Write down your monthly income. After taxes. What actually hits your account.

Now write down your monthly expenses. The whole kit and caboodle. Rent. Transportation. Insurance. Phone. Utilities. Internet. Subscriptions. Debt payments. Gas. Groceries. Eating out. Every last item you actually spend money on every month.

Add them up. For most people reading this, the expenses number is higher than the income number.

That's the gap. The difference between what comes in and what goes out.

The gap compounds and it happens quick. You cover it with credit cards. Credit cards reach limits. Minimum payments increase. Gap widens.

The gap that started small grows larger over time because debt service increases while income stays flat.

That's how you got here. The structural gap slowly destroyed you. Month by month. Compounding.

You cannot build a buffer when you have a gap. The gap drains the buffer faster than you can fill it.

You cannot attack debt when you have a gap. The gap forces you to add new debt while trying to pay off old debt. You cannot save for retirement when you have a gap. The gap consumes every dollar that could go toward the future.

The gap is the primary threat. Everything else waits until you neutralize it.

THE LIFESTYLE EXPANSION

Let's break down what in the world has happened. How did you get here? This is how the gap formed.

Years ago, you made less. Your expenses were less. You had breathing room every month. Not much. But enough.

You got a raise. Income increased. You thought: "Finally. Now I can get ahead."

What happened to the extra money?

Your lifestyle expanded to consume it. You upgraded your phone plan. You added streaming services. You started eating out more. You bought a gym membership. You relaxed your grocery discipline. Small increases across multiple categories.

Within months, expenses matched the new income. Breathing room gone.

Another raise came. "This time I'll save the difference."

Same pattern. Lifestyle expanded. Expenses crept up. Within months, expenses matched income again.

Then life happened. Car needed work. Added to monthly credit card payments. Medical bill added more. Expenses now exceed income.

Income grew over the years. Expenses grew more. The gap opened wider with every raise.

This pattern has a name. In 1955, British naval historian C. Northcote Parkinson published an essay in The Economist identifying a principle he'd observed in bureaucracies: "Work expands to fill the time available for its completion."

Five years later, in his book, The Law and the Profits, Parkinson applied the same principle to money: "Expenditure rises to meet income."

This is Parkinson's Law applied to personal finance. No matter how much your income increases, expenses expand to consume it—unless you actively stop the expansion.

You don't even notice it happening. You just notice that even though you make more money now than you did years ago, you're more stressed and have less margin.

The expansion is automatic. The discipline to stop it isn't.

ECONOMY OF MOTION APPLIED TO EXPENSES

Remember economy of motion from Chapter 2? Every movement must serve the objective or it doesn't happen.

Same principle applies to expenses. Every expense must serve your objective or it gets eliminated.

Right now, your objective is: Close the monthly gap.

Walk through every expense. Ask the question: "Does this serve closing the gap?"

<u>Rent</u>. Serves keeping a roof over your head. Can't eliminate. But could you reduce it? Could you move somewhere cheaper? Could you get a roommate? Maybe. Hold that thought.

Car payment. Serves getting to work. Can't eliminate the car. But could you sell this car and buy a cheaper one with no payment? That eliminates the monthly payment. Accomplishing your goal? Absolutely.

Streaming services. Serves entertainment. Does entertainment serve closing the gap? No. Eliminate.

Gym membership you haven't used in months. Eliminate.

Eating out and coffee runs. Serves convenience and treating yourself. Does that serve closing the gap? No. Cut drastically.

Every expense gets filtered through that question. Serve the objective or get eliminated.

This isn't forever. This is for the next 12—24 months while you close the gap, build the buffer, and attack the debt. Once position is secured, you can add back what matters.

But right now, economy of motion. Every dollar serves the objective of closing the gap.

THE AUSTERE PATH

Einstein wore the same gray suit every day. Same exact suit. He had seven of them in his wardrobe. All identical.

Why?

Because choosing what to wear every morning consumed mental energy. Energy he wanted to spend on physics instead of fashion. So he eliminated the choice. Same suit. Every day. Zero decisions.

That's strategic simplicity. Reducing complexity to conserve resources for what matters.

Monks live in cells. One room. Simple furniture. Minimal possessions. Not because they're punishing themselves. Because simplicity removes distraction from their spiritual practice.

Warriors live in barracks. Minimal gear. It all must serve a function. No extras and nothing decorative. Nothing unnecessary. Because when you're risking your life, you can't waste time or energy managing complexity. There can't be anything that would hinder your efforts in a struggle with those stakes.

Einstein's suits. The monk's cell. The warrior's barracks.

All the same principle: Austere living serves a higher purpose. It's not deprivation. It's strategic allocation of limited resources toward what actually matters.

Right now, you need to live austerely. For the next 12—24 months while you close the gap and build stability.

Austere doesn't mean suffering. It means simple. It means every possession serves a purpose. It means every expense is scrutinized. Go through every obligation. Some you discharge immediately—subscriptions, services you forgot you had, anything optional. What remains is your fixed cost structure

You cut the streaming services. You cancel the gym membership you don't use. You stop eating out. You cook at home. You make coffee at home. You wear clothes you already own until they wear out. You don't buy things unless they're absolutely necessary.

This isn't punishment. This is strategy.

The person drowning in debt while maintaining a lifestyle they can't afford isn't living well. They're drowning.

The person living simply while methodically building position is winning. They just don't look like they're winning to outside observers.

Outside observers don't matter. Winning matters.

DESERVE TRAP

But your brain will be whispering to you as you cut expenses:

"I work hard. I deserve to eat out occasionally."

"I make decent money. I deserve to have streaming services."

"Life is short. I deserve to enjoy it, not just grind constantly."

All of it sounds reasonable. All of it is the deserve trap.

Deserve—thinking destroys position. Every time.

You do work hard. You do make decent money. Life is short.

And you're deep in debt with nothing saved and a monthly gap that's compounding your problem every month.

What you "deserve" doesn't change the math. The math is: you're bleeding monthly. The bleeding must stop before anything else can improve.

The streaming services feel like a small thing. "It's not much. That won't make a real difference."

Correct. That amount alone won't close your gap. But subscriptions, plus unused memberships, plus eating out, plus other convenience purchases add up to a substantial portion of your gap.

Cut them all and you've closed most of your gap just by eliminating things that don't actually serve your life.

The deserve trap is an orientation error in your OODA loop. You're orienting to feelings instead of facts.

Feeling: I deserve these small comforts because I work hard.

Fact: These small comforts cost money every month. That money could close your gap, build your buffer, or attack your debt.

Orient to facts, not feelings. The gap doesn't care about your feelings. The gap responds to math.

THE COMPARISON MECHANISM

The deserve trap doesn't get triggered in a vacuum. It activates when you're looking at something specific that someone else has.

Your daughter's been juggling the soccer ball in the driveway every night for three weeks. Two hundred touches before dinner. She's tracking the travel team's tournament schedule on her phone. Tryouts are next month. $3,200 for the season.

Current available money after all bills and debt payments: $0.

You look at her face. The hope. The excitement. The dream.

You know what you have to say. You've said it before. Different context. Same answer.

"We can't afford it this year. Maybe next year."

Her face falls. She tries to hide the disappointment. Says she understands. Goes to her room.

You sit there knowing that three of her friends from school are playing. Their parents figured it out somehow. They found the money. They made it work.

You couldn't.

Your neighbor's kid plays travel hockey. $4,500 per season. They make it work. Your coworker's daughter went on the school trip to Europe. $2,800. They made it work. Your brother-in-law bought his son a car for his sixteenth birthday. Used, but reliable. $8,000. They made it work.

You can't make any of it work.

Seventy percent of men worry that prices are rising faster than income. Thirty-seven percent worry about covering basic expenses. But the real weight isn't just covering basics. It's the gap between what you provide and what you see others providing. The gap between what your kids need and what their peers have.

The inadequacy — feeling like you're not good enough, not doing enough — is crushing.

That feeling is not the truth about you. It is the weight of caring — about your family, about your role, about doing right by the people depending on you. That caring is strength. But caring doesn't close the gap. And comparison doesn't help you close it. Comparison is the exact mechanism that turns the deserve trap into a financial decision.

PLAYING YOUR FIGHT, NOT THEIRS

In combat, every fighter has a game plan. Their fight. The range they want. The pace they want. The techniques they favor.

The boxer wants to stay at striking range — far enough to punch but not get grabbed. Keep distance. Use superior hand speed and footwork. That's his fight.

The grappler wants to close distance — get in tight. Clinch. Take the fight to the ground. Use superior wrestling and submission skills. That's his fight.

If the boxer gets pulled into clinching range, taken to the ground — he loses. Doesn't matter how good his hands are. He's fighting someone else's fight. If the grappler stays at striking range, tries to outbox — he loses. Doesn't matter how good his ground game is. He's fighting someone else's fight.

The winner is the fighter who imposes their fight. Their range. Their pace. Their strengths.

Your neighbor's financial fight is not your fight.

His income: $140,000. Yours: $68,000. His debt: $0. Yours: $24,000. His housing: inherited house, no payment. Yours: $1,650 monthly rent. Same neighborhood. Different fights. Completely different.

When you compare what you provide to what he provides, you're measuring your fight by his resources. He can afford $4,500 for travel hockey because he's fighting a different fight on different terrain. You're fighting yours. Your income. Your debt. Your obligations.

The travel soccer team isn't your fight. Not this year. Now you're fighting the fight to close the gap. The fight to eliminate debt. The fight to build the buffer. That fight requires all your resources, all your focus, all your effort. You can't fight two fights simultaneously. You can't secure your footing while also matching your neighbor's lifestyle.

Win your fight first. Then — from solid ground — you can afford the extras.

THE COMPARISON LOOP

Here is the exact mechanism that turns comparison into destruction.

You can't afford travel soccer. But the comparison says you should be able to. The inadequacy says you're failing as a provider. The pressure says find the money somehow.

So you find it. Credit card. $3,200 added to existing debt.

Temporary relief. Your daughter plays. You matched the standard. Six months later, you're deeper in the gap. The season ended. The inadequacy returns with the next comparison. Your financial position deteriorated to temporarily match someone else's lifestyle.

You fought their fight instead of yours. You lost.

This is the loop that the deserve trap feeds. You see what others have. Feel inadequate. Pressure builds. You spend to match. Position weakens. Crisis hits. Forced to cut. Build back partial position. See what others have again. Cycle repeats.

Break it by refusing comparison as a valid input for financial decisions. Their fight doesn't inform your fight. Their resources don't measure your adequacy.

NEEDS VERSUS WANTS

Your daughter needs food, shelter, clothing, education, healthcare, safety, love.

She wants travel soccer.

Needs are non-negotiable. Wants are negotiable. You're providing needs. You're succeeding as a provider.

The culture doesn't distinguish between needs and wants. Consumer culture deliberately blurs the line. Marketing exists to make wants feel like needs. "Every kid deserves the opportunity to play travel sports."

No. Every kid deserves food and shelter. Travel sports is a want. A legitimate want. But a want.

The inability to provide wants doesn't equal provider failure. It equals resource allocation during a fight for position.

WHAT YOU'RE ACTUALLY TEACHING THEM

Someone will tell you that you're depriving your children. Family members. Friends. Your spouse potentially. Sometimes your kids themselves.

They mean: "I'm uncomfortable watching you not match the standard I think you should match."

Their discomfort. Not your problem.

Both paths teach lessons. The parent who goes into debt for travel sports while the foundation crumbles is teaching their children that matching social standards matters more than financial stability. That wants justify debt. That comparison drives decisions.

The parent who says "not this year, we're securing position first" is teaching their children that discipline creates options. That delayed gratification serves long-term goals. That fighting your own fight matters more than matching someone else's.

One teaches how to build. One teaches how to break.

Your children don't need you to match the neighbors. They need you to model discipline under pressure. That's not inadequacy. That's the job.

TACTICAL OVERRIDE

You're in week two. The comparison is loudest right now because you're cutting things and you can see clearly what others have that you don't.

The inadequacy will try to send you to a credit card. Don't go there. Instead, go somewhere else entirely.

Find something you can do together that costs nothing. Not for them. With them.

Your daughter wants to play soccer? You can't afford $3,200 for travel team. You can afford zero dollars to go to the park down the street. Bring a ball. Meet her in the driveway. Thirty minutes every evening after dinner — the same thirty minutes she's already out there doing her two hundred touches. She's not waiting for a check. She's waiting for you.

The father who spends $3,200 on travel sports but never plays with his daughter is providing an experience managed by others. The father who can't afford travel sports but meets her in the driveway every evening to kick the ball around is providing presence — there, fully engaged.

Zero dollars. Maximum presence.

Once the presence is handled, pick up the gap work. One move. The noise quiets once you're moving.

TIME BURGLARS

A Time Burglar is a hijacker. They don't just waste your hours; they wrap you up in their problems, their agenda, and their way of thinking until your own mission is buried. When you commit to living austerely to get your financial life back on track, you become a prime target for these thefts.

Your mission requires a specific use of time and a rigid focus on outcomes. The Time Burglar sees that focus and tries to steamroll over it with excuses, taunts, and teasing.

They notice the shift in your lifestyle, and because your discipline makes them uncomfortable, they try to pull you back "in line" with how they think you should live. Each character is cut from the same cloth;

The Coworker: "Come on, man. You deserve a break. It's just lunch." They aren't worried about your hunger; they are hijacking your lunch hour—time you've reclaimed to save money or work on a side hustle —to serve their desire for company.

The Friend: "Seriously? You can't afford $15 for the streaming app?" This is a taunt. They are trying to get you to adopt their "small luxury" mindset, forcing you to defend your math instead of pursuing your goal.

The Family Member: "You're being cheap. You can afford a gift." This is a guilt-trip agenda. They are trying to make their holiday traditions more comfortable by sacrificing your financial recovery.

These are strategies of the steal that Time Burglars employ. They are trying to redirect your focus from your mission to their place of comfort. They use "teasing" to make your austerity look like a character flaw, but it's actually a power move. They want you doing what they want you to do—which ultimately serves zero interest of yours.

Their discomfort with your mission is not your problem.

Your objective is closing the gap and building a position of strength. Their opinion of that objective does not serve the outcome. When they attempt to pull you into their way of thinking, you have two responses:

Response One: The Silent Wall. Ignore the comment completely. Do not explain your budget. Do not justify your lack of a gift. Do not defend your "cheapness." When you explain, you are handing them the keys to your time. Just move forward.

Response Two: The Plain Facts. State your position without seeking approval: "I'm focused on closing a monetary gap and building a position for my future. This is how I'm doing it." Then stop talking. Do not try to convince them that austerity is good. Do not ask them to understand. You don't need their validation; you need them to stop hijacking your focus.

Time Burglars steal your attention from the objective. They want you living on their terms, spending on their schedule, and worrying about their feelings. Don't let them.

BALANCE IS A LUXURY

"You need work—life balance."

"You can't grind forever."

"You need to take care of your mental health."

All true. All important. All luxuries you can't afford right now.

Balance is something you maintain after you've solid ground. Not before.

Right now, you're not in position. You're drowning. Asking someone who's drowning to maintain balance is asking them to drown with good form.

First, you get to shore. Then you think about balance.

The next 12—24 months are imbalanced. Deliberately. Strategically. You're allocating all available resources toward closing the gap, building the buffer, attacking the debt.

Not because balance doesn't matter. Because imbalance now serves balance later.

The person who maintains perfect balance while drowning eventually drowns.

The person who accepts strategic imbalance, gets to shore, then achieves balance from stable ground wins.

You're getting to shore first. Balance comes after.

SOP: THIS MINUTE

Write down your three biggest expenses that can be eliminated,

We are looking for extras, anything unnecessary.

Three things. Write them down now.

SOP: THIS WEEK

You're going to cut those three expenses. Not reduce them. Cut them completely.

Monday: Identify the three expenses from THIS MINUTE. Write down what they are and how much they cost monthly.

Tuesday: Cancel or eliminate the first expense. Subscription? Cancel it. Membership? Cancel it. Habit? Stop it. Do it today. Get confirmation.

Wednesday: Cancel or eliminate the second expense. Same process. Today.

Thursday: Cancel or eliminate the third expense. All three gone by end of day Thursday.

Friday: Calculate the monthly savings. Add up the three expenses you cut. Write it down. That's your gap reduction.

Saturday: Identify three more expenses you could cut. Smaller ones probably. But three more. Write them down.

Sunday: Review your week. Three expenses cut. Money per month freed up. That money doesn't go to lifestyle. It goes to closing the gap. Set up automatic transfer if possible. If not, manual transfer every payday.

By end of week, you've reduced your monthly expenses substantially. That's meaningful progress toward closing the gap in seven days.

SOP: THIS MONTH

Week one: run this WEEK. Cut three major expenses. Redirect savings to gap.

Week two: Cut three more expenses. Smaller ones. Every dollar counts. Redirect to gap.

Week three: Review every remaining expense. Can rent be reduced? Can you move somewhere cheaper or get a roommate? Can the car payment be eliminated by selling and buying cheaper with cash? Can insurance be reduced by shopping around? Can utilities be cut by changing habits? Attack in all directions. Find more to cut.

Week four: Calculate total gap closed this month. You started with a gap. You cut expenses in week one. Cut more in week two. Cut more in week three. Your gap is substantially smaller. Possibly closed completely.

Month two: Attack any remaining gap. Find it. Cut it. Close the gap completely.

By end of month two, income equals or exceeds expenses. Gap closed. The bleeding stops.

Now you can build the buffer without it draining. Now you can attack debt without adding new debt. Now forward progress becomes possible.

But only after the gap closes.

TACTICAL OVERRIDE

You're in week two. You're supposed to be cutting three more expenses.

You can't. You're attached to these things. Emotionally attached. They're part of your identity. Part of who you are.

The extra backpacks and sports bags that just take up an extra bin.

The camera equipment you upgraded to. You're a photographer. Selling it means admitting you're not pursuing that passion.

The tools in the garage. You're a builder. Selling them means giving up that part of yourself.

This is the Linus Blanket problem. The attachment to possessions as identity.

Stop thinking about what these items mean to you. Start thinking about what they're costing you.

Miyamoto Musashi wrote: "Think lightly of yourself and deeply of the world." And: "Do nothing which is of no use."

Here's the plan:

You sell the bike for $400. That money closes part of your gap. Creates breathing room. In two years, when position is secured and you actually have time and resources to ride regularly, you buy a 2027 model. Better technology. Lighter. Faster. Upgraded components.

If you haven't used it in six months, you're not using it. Sell it. Free up the cash. Close the gap.

When you're positioned to actually pursue those interests from stable ground, you buy better equipment and actually use it.

This is Sun Tzu: Giving up untenable ground. Retreating to defensible position. Then counterattacking from strength.

You can't defend every position simultaneously. You're overextended. Pull back to core position. Defend that. Then expand from strength.

Sell the things you're not using. Close the gap. build stability. Then re—acquire what matters from stable ground.

Tactical repositioning serves strategic victory.

KEY ELEMENTS

Economy of motion: Every dollar serves closing the gap or it doesn't get spent. Every possession serves your current life or it gets sold. No wasted motion.

Austere path: Einstein's suits. Monk's cell. Warrior's barracks. Strategic simplicity serving higher purpose. Not deprivation. Strategic allocation of limited resources toward what matters.

WHAT'S NEXT

The month that never arrives—the clean month, the one where nothing goes wrong and the timing lines up—that month doesn't exist. It never did, and sadly never will. What exists instead is a structural gap that grows a little wider every time a bill goes on a card and a minimum payment goes up. Why? Because the SOP running your money is the same one that got you here. You keep doing the same things and expecting different results.

The relief you felt with the last raise, and then the confusion about where it went, wasn't a spending problem. It was a system problem. The SOP consumed it because you didn't have a different system ready to catch it.

The gap closes before anything else can be built. That's the sequence. The next chapter is the third of the seven battles—and it's the one that's probably costing you the most in interest right now.

CHAPTER 5
DEBT QUICKSAND

"In fighting and in everyday life you should be determined though calm."

- Miyamoto Musashi

You have debt across multiple accounts.

Credit cards. Medical bills. Personal loans. Different balances. Different interest rates. Different minimum payments.

Total minimum payments across all accounts consume a substantial portion of your monthly income.

You've been making minimum payments for months. Maybe years.

The balances aren't moving.

Look at one of your accounts from six months ago compared to now. You've paid hundreds or thousands in minimum payments. The balance barely dropped. Maybe it even increased.

Most of your payment went to interest—the extra money they charge you for borrowing. Very little went to debt reduction.

At this rate, paying minimums only, you'll have this debt paid off in approximately two decades. You'll pay roughly double what you actually borrowed when you total the principal and all the accumulated interest.

Twenty—plus years. Double the original amount. To pay off debt you've already spent.

That's the quicksand. You're stuck. Making payments but not escaping. The debt pulls you down while you fight to stay in place.

ESCAPE FROM INFERIOR POSITION

In Brazilian Jiu—Jitsu, there's a position called the mount. Your opponent is on top of you. Chest to chest. Their weight pressing down. You're pinned. They control the fight.

This is called an inferior position. You're losing. They're winning. Every second you stay there, you're in danger.

New students panic. They try to explode out using maximum strength. Push with all they have. Trying to throw the opponent off through sheer force.

Doesn't work. The opponent is positioned. They have leverage. Your explosive strength gets smothered. You burn all your energy in thirty seconds. Now you're exhausted and still pinned.

You lost not because you weren't strong enough. You lost because you used the wrong escape method.

The systematic escape works differently.

Step one: Stop adding more problems. The opponent wants you to panic. Wants you to make mistakes. Wants you to give up your back or expose your neck. Don't. Stay calm. Protect yourself. Stop making it worse.

Step two: Create space. Not through explosion. Through technique. Insert a frame—using your elbow and arm to create a small barrier between you and the opponent. Just inches of space. Doesn't look like much. But it's going to make all the difference.

Step three: Create space. Hip escape. Move your hips a few inches. Then a few more. Then more. Slowly extracting yourself from underneath. Each small movement improving your footing slightly.

Small, subtle and systematic maneuvers.

Three minutes later, you're out from under mount. Using patience, determination and strategy. Through technique and an "If This, Then That" system.

Your debt is the mount. You're pinned under $31,400. Minimum payments are your exhausted thrashing that burns energy without escaping.

The systematic escape works the same way the Jiu—Jitsu escape works.

Stop adding new debt. Create space through freeing up payments. Escape tactics are to target and attack debts smallest to largest.

THE FRAME

Step one: Stop adding new debt.

This is the frame. In grappling, the frame creates space so you can start escaping. In debt elimination, the frame is the commitment to add no new debt while you're escaping.

If you're attacking debt while simultaneously adding new debt, you're staying in the same position. Maybe getting worse.

That's trying to escape mount while your opponent keeps resetting your base.

The frame means: No new debt added. Period.

Emergency happens? Three options that don't break the frame:

Option one: Negotiate with the vendor. Medical bill? Call them. "I can pay $50 monthly until it's paid off." Most will accept payment plans.

Option two: Temporarily reduce your debt attack. Attacking Credit Card 1 with $200 extra this month? Emergency hits. Reduce attack to $100. Use the other $100 for the emergency. Still attacking debt, just slower this month.

Option three: Generate additional income. Covered in Chapter 3. Pick up extra work. Sell unused items. Generate the cash you need without adding debt.

What you don't do: Add new credit card debt. That breaks the frame. That resets your base while you're trying to escape.

The frame must hold. No new debt. Whatever it takes.

HIP ESCAPES (DEBT SNOWBALL)

Step two: Escape using the debt snowball method.

You list all debts smallest to largest by total balance. Write them out. Smallest at the top. Largest at the bottom.

Now you attack them in exactly that order. Smallest first. Largest last.

Pay minimums on anything except the smallest debt. Attack the smallest debt with every extra dollar you can generate.

How much extra can you attack with? You closed your monthly gap in Chapter 4. That freed up money. You built your buffer to $500 in Chapter 3. Buffer is set. Now that freed—up money can attack debt.

Take your minimum payment on the smallest debt. Add all the extra money you freed up from closing the gap. That total amount attacks the smallest debt every month.

Plan: Divide the balance by your monthly attack amount. That tells you how many months until that first debt is eliminated.

A few months from now, the first debt is eliminated. Completely gone.

Now you take that entire payment amount and redirect it to the next smallest debt.

Second debt gets attacked by its minimum payment plus the extra you freed up from eliminating the first debt.

Timeline: Balance divided by new monthly attack amount. Shows you when this debt dies.

Each debt you eliminate frees up its payment. That freed payment gets added to the attack on the next debt. The amount attacking debt grows with each victory.

You keep going. Third debt. Fourth debt. Fifth debt. Each one falls faster than the last because your monthly attack power keeps growing.

Committed from start to finish: A few years of consistent action eliminates all debt. Compared to two decades paying minimums.

That's the debt snowball. Each payment you free up gets added to the attack on the next debt. The amount attacking debt grows. The momentum compounds. The snowball gets bigger as it rolls.

WHY SMALLEST FIRST

You might be thinking: "But my highest—interest debt should be attacked first to save money on interest, right?"

Mathematically, yes. Attacking highest interest first saves you some money in total interest over the payoff period compared to attacking smallest first.

But you won't do it.

Here's why: Attacking highest interest first often means attacking your largest balance first. At normal attack amounts, that takes years just to finish the first debt.

Years of attacking debt without seeing a single account go to zero. Years of effort before one victory.

Most people quit before they see results. They don't see progress. They don't feel momentum. They get demoralized and stop.

Attacking smallest first means victory in months. First debt eliminated. You see an account disappear. You feel progress. You get momentum.

Within the first year, multiple accounts are gone. You're getting consistent wins. Consistent reinforcement that the SOP works. Consistent proof that you're escaping.

Psychology beats math every time in crushing your debts. You need wins to maintain motivation. Small wins compound into momentum. Momentum carries you through the full itinerary.

The person who optimizes for maximum interest savings but quits halfway through still has all their debt plus accumulated interest. They saved nothing. They're still drowning.

The person who pays slightly more in total interest but eliminates all debt is debt—free. They won.

Smallest first. Get the wins. Build the momentum. Stay in the fight until you've won.

THE COMPOUND EFFECT

Let's examine a best case timetable that has real momentum:

Early months: First debt eliminated. One down, several to go. First win. Proof it works.

First year: Second debt eliminated. You're making real progress by number of accounts. Momentum building.

Midpoint: Third debt eliminated. More than halfway done by number of accounts. You can see the end.

Late stage: Fourth debt eliminated. Almost there. Final push.

Final months: Last debt eliminated. All debt gone. Zero balances across all accounts. The money that was going to debt payments is now freed up.

Compare that to paying minimums:

Year 5: All balances barely moved. You've paid tens of thousands total. Balances reduced by only a fraction. Still owe most of the debt. Many more years to go. You're exhausted and want to quit.

Year 10: Still making minimum payments. You've paid enormous amounts total. Balances reduced but still substantial debt remaining. Years more to go if you can maintain it.

Year 17+: Finally paid off. Total paid: multiple times what you originally borrowed when you add all the interest.

But most people don't make it 17 years. They quit. They declare bankruptcy. They get crushed.

The snowball method: A few years to freedom. Reasonable total interest paid. Versus two decades and massive interest.

The systematic approach wins because it accounts for human psychology, not just math.

THE PSYCHOLOGICAL WEIGHT

Debt isn't just numbers on a screen. It's psychological weight you carry every day.

Having debt means:

You avoid checking your accounts because seeing the balances triggers anxiety. So you don't check. So you don't really know where you stand. So the anxiety gets worse.

You feel shame when people talk about money. You feel like you're failing at something basic. You feel like everyone else has it figured out except you.

That discomfort means you care. The people who never feel it aren't better with money—they're just less honest with themselves. You're already ahead of where you think you are.

You avoid social situations that cost money because you can't afford them. But you can't tell people why. So you make excuses. So you feel isolated.

You snap at your spouse over small things because you're carrying stress you can't release. The debt is creating tension in your relationship even when you're not talking about debt.

That's the psychological weight. It's not proportional to the dollar amount. Smaller debts create just as much stress as larger ones because all debt represents failure and shame and being trapped.

Each debt eliminated removes disproportionate psychological weight.

First debt eliminated? That's not just money reduced. That's one account that's no longer sitting in the back of your mind creating stress. That's one less password to remember. One less login to avoid. One less source of shame.

By the time you've eliminated multiple accounts, the psychological weight doesn't decrease linearly. It decreases exponentially. Multiple accounts gone feels like massive weight lifted even though you've only paid a fraction of your total debt.

That's why smallest first works psychologically. Each eliminated account feels like a massive win even if the dollar amount is small.

SOP: THIS MINUTE

List all your debts smallest to largest by total balance owed.

Don't estimate. Don't guess. Log into each account. Write down the exact current balance.

Then write them in order:

Debt 1 (smallest): ______ Debt 2: ______ Debt 3: ______ Debt 4: ______ Debt 5 (largest): ______

That's your attack order. Smallest to largest. That's the sequence.

SOP: THIS WEEK

Monday: Verify the minimum payment on each debt. Log in to each account. Write down the minimum required payment for each.

Tuesday: Calculate how much you can attack debt with beyond minimums. You closed the gap in Chapter 4. How much monthly did that free up? That's your debt attack amount.

Wednesday: Set up automatic payments for minimum amounts on every debt except the smallest. Automate the minimums so you never miss one. Prevents late fees and credit damage.

Thursday: Calculate your attack power on the smallest debt. Minimum payment plus extra attack amount. That total attacks the smallest debt every month.

Friday: Calculate timeline to eliminate smallest debt. Divide balance by monthly attack amount. That's your first victory finish line.

Saturday: Set up your attack payment for next month. Manual payment or automatic, whatever works. But get it scheduled. First attack payment goes out within seven days.

Sunday: Review your plan. All minimums automated. First debt being attacked with every bit of extra cash and coins. Schedule calculated. You know exactly when that first debt dies.

SOP: THIS MONTH

Week one: run this WEEK. All minimums automated. Attack payment scheduled.

Week two: First attack payment executes. Smallest debt balance drops. Track it. Write down the new balance. You're moving.

Week three: Look for additional money to attack debt faster. Can you generate extra money this month? Extra work? Sell one more item? Every extra dollar shortens the distance to the finish line.

Week four: Second attack payment executes. Calculate progress. Your smallest debt balance has dropped substantially from two attack payments. You can see it dying. You can feel momentum. This is working.

By month's end, smallest debt is substantially reduced. You can see it dying. You can feel momentum. This is working.

WHAT'S NEXT

The minimum payment on each account is designed to keep you in the relationship as long as possible, not to get you out of it. Paying minimums on everything for another decade is a choice, even if it never felt like one. So is targeting the smallest balance first and closing accounts one by one until the payments that used to go to creditors go to you.

The math on the snowball method is real. The psychological weight of the first account hitting zero is real in a different way—and that second kind of real is what carries people through month seventeen when the motivation is long gone.

Every debt you eliminate frees a payment. That freed payment doesn't disappear—it becomes attack power for the next debt, and eventually, it becomes the capacity to fight a different battle entirely.

Because here's what debt has been doing beyond the interest charges and the minimum payments: it's been occupying the ground where your future should be standing. Every dollar bleeding to a creditor is a dollar not compounding for sixty-year-old you. You've been fighting the present battle so hard the future battle became invisible.

You can see it now. The debt is moving. The sequence is working. And the moment you look up from the snowball—from the accounts closing one by one—there's something else on the horizon you've been avoiding looking at directly.

The retirement account you haven't opened in two years. The number that makes the calculator give up.

That's the next battle. And the same system that just started winning this one is going to win that one too.

CHAPTER 6
THE CALCULATOR QUIT

"It is better to have one friend of great value than many friends who are good for nothing." - Miyamoto Musashi

You're 47 years old.

You just logged into your retirement account for the first time in two years. You've been avoiding it. Scared to look. Because deep down you already know what you're going to see.

The balance loads. Your stomach drops. It's a fraction of what you need.

You try different scenarios. What if you contribute more? What if you work longer? What if the market performs better than average? You run the numbers twenty different ways.

Every scenario leads to the same conclusion: The gap between what you have and what you need is insurmountable. The path to working until you physically collapse feels inevitable.

You close the laptop. Pour a drink. And tell yourself you'll figure it out later. Same thing you told yourself two years ago when you last checked the balance.

But later never comes. The gap just gets wider.

I want to put emphasis on something right now: The problem isn't the gap. The problem is the SOP that created it.

THE ACTUAL PROBLEM

You think the problem is that you started late. That if you'd started contributing twenty years ago, you'd be fine. That the issue is time you can't get back.

Wrong.

Starting late is a factor, sure. But it's not the actual problem. Plenty of people start late and still retire with security. They're not superheroes. They're not making massive incomes. They're just executing a system that works.

The problem is this: You've been operating on sporadic heroics instead of sustained systematic contributions.

Let's pretend: You get a bonus at work. You're feeling good. You dump the whole thing into your retirement account. Heroic contribution. You feel like you're making progress. Maybe you are, for that one month.

Then what happens? Nothing. For months. Sometimes a whole year. No contributions. The account just sits there. You meant to contribute regularly. You really did. But there was always something else. The car broke down. The kids needed something. Bills piled up. Life happened.

Then you get another raise. Or a tax refund. And you do it again. Heroic contribution. Feeling good for a moment. Then back to nothing.

You're trying to save for retirement the same way an untrained fighter tries to win a fight—with random bursts of maximum effort followed by complete collapse. No system. No sustainability. Just desperation and adrenaline.

And what happens to that fighter? They lose. Every time. Because a system that depends on motivation always fails.

Think about what happens to the money that should have gone to retirement. You get a raise. Where does it go? Lifestyle expansion. Bigger apartment. Nicer car. Better restaurants. More subscriptions. The raise disappears into your standard of living within months.

You get a bonus. Where does it go? Maybe some to retirement, like we said. But the rest? New TV. Vacation you've been putting off. Clothes you've been wanting. Stuff. Always stuff. The bonus evaporates.

Every windfall becomes immediate consumption instead of systematic allocation. Every bit of extra money finds somewhere else to go. And your retirement account stays where it is—barely moving, definitely not growing enough.

The problem isn't the numbers. It's the broken system that produces sporadic effort. And broken systems produce broken results.

TRAINING FOR THE LONG FIGHT

In combat, there are two completely different types of fights. The short fight and the long fight. Different durations require completely different approaches. Get this wrong and you lose before the fight even starts.

The short fight lasts maybe thirty seconds. Maybe a minute. It's explosive. It's violent. It's maximum intensity from the first second to the last. You empty the gas tank and exhaust yourself. Every ounce of energy. Every bit of power. You're not conserving anything because there's nothing to conserve for. The fight will be over before you know it.

Sprint pace. All—out effort. Finish it fast or get finished fast. That's the short fight.

Now the long fight. Five rounds. Twenty—five minutes. Maybe longer if it goes to a decision. Try to fight that at sprint pace and you're done in round one. Gassed. Flat on your back. Arms too heavy to lift. Lungs screaming. Brain hypoxic. Easy target for anyone who paced themselves properly.

The long fight demands sustainable output. You manage your breathing. You pick your moments. You don't throw every combination at maximum power because you'll need that power in round four. You use technique to conserve energy. You make your opponent work harder than you work. You build a system that can function for the full duration.

And here's the thing about retirement: It's not a short fight. It's not even a long fight by combat standards. Retirement is a twenty to forty year fight. From when you start saving seriously to when you actually need the money. Steely up, I said this will be a decades long struggle.

You can't sprint a twenty—year projection. Nobody can. Try it and you collapse. You burn out. You quit. You revert to old patterns. The SOP fails because it was never designed to sustain permanently.

What wins the long fight? Sustainable system. Not heroic effort. Not maximum intensity when you're feeling motivated. Sustainable consistent action that functions whether you're motivated or not.

Small consistent contributions beat large sporadic contributions every single time. Not because of motivation. Not because of discipline. Because of math. Because of how compound growth actually works. Because sustainability beats intensity over long timelines.

You're training for a fight that lasts decades. Train accordingly. Build a system you can maintain when you're tired. When you're broke. When you're unmotivated. When life is falling apart. Because those moments will come. And your system needs to function anyway.

And you are already in training. Reading this is training. Understanding the SOP is training. The work has begun—even if it doesn't feel like it yet.

THE COMPOUND TRUTH

A common misconception about compound growth is not with the specific numbers—those change based on market conditions and account types and a thousand variables. But with the principle that never changes.

Two people save the exact same total amount of money over thirty years. Same total contributions. Same account type. Same investments. Identical except for one thing: timing.

Person A contributes small amounts every single month for thirty years. Consistent. Systematic. Never misses a month. Never stops. Just keeps feeding the account month after month after month.

Person B contributes in bursts. Big chunks when they feel motivated or when money comes in. Then nothing for months. Then another big contribution. Sporadic. Irregular. But over thirty years, they contribute the same total amount as Person A. Same money in. Just different timing.

At the end of thirty years, their account balances are dramatically different. This is very important; Person A has substantially more money. Not a little more. Substantially more. Sometimes double. Sometimes more than double. Do you see the difference this makes?

Same money contributed. Completely different results.

Why? Because compound growth rewards time in the market more than amount in the market. Time in the market always wins. The money Person A contributed in year one has been compounding for thirty years. Every contribution compounds for the full remaining timeline. Maximum time equals maximum growth.

Person B's sporadic contributions don't get the same compounding time. Some contributions compound for years. Others for months. The growth is inconsistent because the SOP is inconsistent. They break the compounding cycle every time they stop contributing. They lose months or years of growth they can never recover.

Here's another way to think about it. Compound growth doesn't just work on your contributions. It works on the growth itself. Your money makes money. Then that new money makes money. Then that money makes money. It's exponential, not linear.

But exponential growth needs time to work. Interrupt the SOP and you interrupt the compounding. The growth resets. You're starting from a lower base. You lose the momentum that was building.

Every month you skip is a month of compound growth you'll never get back. And you don't get those dollars or that opportunity back. Because compound growth works on time, and time only moves forward.

The people who retire with substantial accounts aren't the ones who made heroic contributions. They're the ones who made consistent contributions. They understood that consistency beats intensity when you're fighting a decades—long battle.

Compound growth is a weapon. But only if you use it correctly. And correct use means consistent action over the full agenda. Not sporadic bursts when you feel like it.

WHY PEOPLE FAIL

Retirement contributions feel optional. That's the first problem.

The electric bill isn't optional. Skip it and the lights go out this month. The rent isn't optional. Skip it and you're evicted next month. The car payment isn't optional. Skip it and they repo it within weeks. Immediate consequences. Visible consequences. Painful consequences.

But retirement? Skip the contribution this month and nothing happens. No lights turn off. No eviction notice. No repo man. Life continues exactly the same. The consequences are twenty or thirty years away. Maybe longer. Too far away to feel real. Too far away to create urgency.

So when money gets tight, retirement contributions get cut. Every time. Because cutting something with distant consequences is easier than cutting something with immediate consequences. Your brain prioritizes survival today over security decades from now.

That's problem one. Retirement feels optional because the consequences are invisible.

Problem two: The numbers feel impossible.

You look at where you are now. You look at where you need to be. The gap is so massive that your brain can't even process a realistic path from here to there. It's not that the path is hard. It's that the path is invisible.

When you can't see the path, you don't take the first step. You stand there running calculations. Trying to find the perfect strategy. Waiting for clarity that never comes. Paralyzed by a problem that feels unsolvable.

Meanwhile time keeps moving. The gap gets wider. The problem gets worse. And you're still standing there doing nothing.

Problem three: Waiting for capacity.

You tell yourself you'll start contributing seriously when you have more capacity. When you get the raise. When the debt is paid off. When the kids are older and expenses drop. When you're in a better position financially.

Those conditions never arrive. There's always another expense. Another emergency. Another reason to wait. Perfect conditions don't exist. You're waiting for something that will never come.

Meanwhile, people with less income than you are building retirement accounts. They're not waiting for capacity. They're using current capacity and growing it as they go. They started with what they had. Then they increased as capacity increased. But they started.

You're still waiting.

The Game Plan: Start with current capacity. Whatever you can contribute right now, contribute it. Every single dollar counts at this stage, because it is setting your trajectory.

Then grow the contribution as capacity grows. Get a raise? Increase the contribution before lifestyle expands to consume it. Pay off a debt?

Redirect that payment to retirement. Build capacity over time instead of waiting for it to appear magically.

The SOP that works is simple: Start now with what you have. Never stop. Never revert. Accomplish this for decades until position is secured. That's it. That's the whole system.

THE SMALL PERCENTAGE PRINCIPLE

Start with a small percentage of your gross income. Two to three percent. That's it. You can find that amount. I don't care how tight your budget is. You can find two to three percent. One or two small cuts.

But here's the critical part: You don't stay there.

Two to three percent is your starting point, not your ending point. It's the base you build from. Once the SOP is running, you increase. As capacity grows, the percentage grows.

Here's what that looks like over time. Year one: Two to three percent. You're getting used to the contribution. Building the habit. Proving to yourself that the SOP works. The amount is small but it's consistent. You're in the fight.

Year two or three: You've paid off a couple small debts. Freed up some monthly cash flow. Redirect half of it to retirement. Now you're contributing four or five percent. Still sustainable. Still manageable. But growing.

Year five: More debts eliminated. Maybe got a raise. You're living on less than you make consistently now. Lifestyle hasn't expanded. Redirect the freed capacity to retirement. Now you're at six or seven percent. Real money starting to accumulate. Compound growth building momentum.

Year ten: All consumer debt gone. Substantial percentage of income going to retirement. Maybe ten or twelve percent. Maybe more. The account balance is significant now. You can see the path. You can project the outcome. You're going to make it.

That's how you bridge the gap. Not with heroic contributions that can't be sustained. With small systematic increases over a long timetable. The percentage grows. The contribution grows. The balance compounds. The future becomes secure.

Most people do it backwards. They wait until they can contribute ten or fifteen percent before starting. So they never start. Or they start at ten percent, can't sustain it, and quit within months. Back to zero.

Start small. Increase slowly with precision. Sustain indefinitely. That's what works.

Two to three percent right now is infinitely more valuable than fifteen percent someday. Because someday never comes. Right now is all you have.

THE AGE MYTH

"I'm too old to start now."

I hear this from people in their forties. Their fifties. Sometimes their thirties. They've convinced themselves that starting late means it's pointless. That the opportunity has passed. That they've already lost the retirement fight before it even started.

This is a paralyzing lie your brain tells you to avoid the discomfort of starting.

Let's define what "too old" actually means. Too old to start means you have zero years left to compound growth. Too old means you're retiring tomorrow and have no time to build anything. That's too old. That's when starting doesn't help.

You're not retiring tomorrow. You've got fifteen years. Twenty years. Maybe twenty—five years before you need this money. That's not zero time. That's substantial compounding time.

Is it as much time as someone who started at twenty—five? No. Obviously not. But it's enough time to build real security if you perform the plan properly. It's enough time for compound growth to work its magic. It's enough time to go from nothing to something substantial.

You know what happens if you don't start because you think you're too old? In fifteen years you'll be fifteen years older with nothing saved. Zero security. Complete dependence on working until you physically can't. That's the outcome of believing the age myth.

You know what happens if you start today despite feeling old? In fifteen years you'll be fifteen years older with a retirement account that's been compounding for fifteen years. Real money. Real security. Real options. That's the outcome of rejecting the age myth and executing anyway.

Both timelines happen. The only difference is whether you acted or stayed paralyzed. Whether you started or kept waiting. Whether you fought or surrendered.

Here's another truth that's hard to hear: Every year you wait costs you years of compound growth. Not months. Years. Because compound growth is exponential. The earlier contributions compound for longer and produce disproportionate returns. Delay one year and you don't just lose one year of contributions—you lose all the compound growth those contributions would have generated over the remaining timeline.

The cost of delay accelerates. Wait five years and you've lost more than five years of growth. Wait ten and you've lost more than ten years. The math gets worse the longer you wait.

So what do you do with that information? You could let it paralyze you further. Convince yourself it's too late. Give up completely. Or you could let it motivate you to start right now. This minute. Before you lose another day.

Or you could start this minute. Right now. Before finishing this page. The gap between those two choices is not willpower—it's a decision. And decisions happen in a second.

One more thing about age. You're going to get older whether you save for retirement or not. Time doesn't stop because you're scared. In fifteen years you'll be fifteen years older. That's guaranteed. The only question is whether you'll be fifteen years older with security or fifteen years older with nothing.

Mortality awareness should motivate you, not paralyze you. You have limited time. Use it. Don't waste it on the myth that you've already lost. You haven't lost until you quit. Start now. Fight now. Win what's still winnable.

THE AUSTERE ADVANTAGE

Here's something that nobody wants to hear but everyone needs to understand: The people who retire comfortably lived below their means for decades.

They didn't expand their lifestyle to match their income. Ever. They got raises and lived on the same amount they were living on before. The raise went to retirement. Disciplined, intelligent, smart, not lucky!

They drove used cars while making enough to buy new ones. They lived in modest homes while making enough for bigger ones. They cooked at home while making enough to eat out constantly. They said no to lifestyle inflation while everyone around them said yes.

And here's the part that makes most people uncomfortable: This isn't temporary.

This isn't "live below your means until you pay off debt then go back to normal." This is a lifestyle. A permanent approach to money. Living below your means isn't a phase you go through. It's the foundation of financial security.

Most people treat austerity like a diet. Something you do temporarily to achieve a goal, then quit once you hit the goal. They sacrifice for a few years, build some security, then reward themselves by increasing spending. Back to old patterns. Back to living at or above their means. And the security they built starts eroding.

The people who win the long fight understand that austere living isn't punishment. It's strategy. It's choosing freedom later over consumption now. It's choosing security over status. It's choosing position over appearance.

Simple living now equals financial freedom later. That's the trade. And it's not even a bad trade. You sacrifice stuff you don't need for security you desperately need. You sacrifice impressing people who don't matter for freedom that matters more than anything.

Think about what financial freedom actually means. It means you can walk away from jobs you hate. It means you can take risks on opportunities without betting your survival. It means emergencies don't destroy you. It means you're not dependent on anyone or anything beyond your control.

That freedom costs something. It costs lifestyle. It costs consumption. It costs keeping up with everyone else. But those costs are nothing compared to what you gain.

Austere living is a weapon. Used properly, it builds freedom nobody can take from you. Used improperly—or not used at all—you stay dependent and vulnerable forever. Choose the weapon. Choose the freedom. Choose the austere path.

THE DEBT—RETIREMENT BALANCE

You've got debt. You need to build retirement. You can't do both at maximum intensity. So what do you do?

Most people pick one and ignore the other. Either they attack debt exclusively and contribute nothing to retirement, or they build retirement and ignore debt.

Start with this strategic approach: Seek high interest debt first and DESTROY it.

First priority: If your employer offers matching contributions on retirement accounts, get the match. This is free money. Your employer contributes money to your retirement account based on what you contribute. Refusing the match is leaving money on the table. Don't leave money on the table.

Contribute enough to get the full match. Not more. Just enough for the match. That's your baseline retirement contribution. Lock it in. Never touch it. Let that run automatically no matter what.

Second priority: Attack high—interest debt with extreme prejudice. Credit cards charging double—digit interest rates. Payday loans. Any debt where the interest rate is destroying you. Kill those first. All extra money after the retirement match goes to high—interest debt until it's eliminated.

Why? Because paying double—digit interest while trying to build retirement is fighting against yourself. The interest you're paying costs more than the growth you're earning. You're running in place. Maybe running backwards. Kill the high—interest debt and you stop the bleeding.

Third priority: Once high—interest debt is gone, split your attack power. Half to remaining debt. Half to retirement. You're fighting two battles simultaneously now, but neither battle is charging you ruinous interest anymore. Both are winnable.

As each debt gets eliminated, redirect that payment. Where does it go? Split it. Half to the next debt in line. Half to retirement. Your debt attack power grows. Your retirement contribution grows. Both systems accelerate.

Final stage: All debt eliminated. Now all that money that was going to debt goes to retirement. You've been living without that money for years. Your lifestyle is already adjusted. Don't expand it now. Redirect the full amount to retirement. Watch the balance grow.

This is the systematic approach. Employer match first. High—interest debt second. Split allocation third. Full retirement contributions fourth. Each stage builds on the previous stage. The SOP compounds on itself.

You don't choose between debt and retirement. You fight both battles strategically. Prioritize properly. Discharge in orderly fashion. Win both fights completely.

SOP: THIS MINUTE

Calculate two to three percent of your gross income. Not your take—home pay. Your gross income—the amount before taxes and deductions.

Write that number down. Physically write it. Don't just think about it. Don't just remember it. Write it on paper where you can see it.

That's your starting point. That's the amount you're committing to contribute every single month. Without exception. Without negotiation. Without reverting.

That's your move this minute. Calculate. Write. Commit. Done.

SOP: THIS WEEK

Day one: Research where to open a retirement account. Don't spend days on this. An hour. Maybe two. Find a simple provider with low fees and straightforward options. Simple beats perfect. Movement beats analysis.

Day two: Open the account. Online application. Twenty minutes. Maybe less. Answer the questions. Choose the simplest investment option available. Don't overthink it. Done.

Day three: Set up the automatic contribution. Connect your bank account. Schedule the monthly transfer. Use the number you calculated in This Minute. Make it automatic so it happens whether you remember it or not.

Day four: Adjust your budget to accommodate the contribution. Find the two to three percent. Cut something. Cancel something. Reduce something. Make the math work. The money has to come from somewhere. Find it.

Day five: Verify the first contribution is scheduled. Check the account. Confirm the automatic transfer is set up correctly. Make sure the SOP is running. First contribution should begin within the next month.

That's your week. Five days. Five specific actions. By the end of the week you have an account open, contributions scheduled, and a system running automatically. Position established. Fight engaged.

SOP: THIS MONTH

Week one: First contribution executes. Money moves from your account to your retirement account automatically. The SOP is working. You're in the fight.

Week two: Don't obsess over the balance. Don't log in every day to check how much it's grown. It's been two weeks. It hasn't grown much. That's fine. This is a long fight. Stop checking.

Week three: Review your budget. Is the contribution sustainable? Are you actually living on less to accommodate it? If not, make more cuts. If yes, good. System is stable.

Week four: Set a reminder to check the account quarterly. Every three months. That's frequent enough to monitor progress without obsessing over daily fluctuations.

If you paid off a debt this month or got a raise, increase the contribution immediately. Don't wait. Don't let the extra capacity get absorbed into lifestyle. Redirect it now while it's still available.

That's your month. System running automatically. Contributions executing without intervention. Balance growing through compound interest. You're executing the plan. Position improving. Fight progressing.

TACTICAL OVERRIDE

You're paralyzed by account options. Too many choices. Too many investment strategies. Too much information. You're researching for weeks trying to find the optimal account and the optimal strategy.

Stop.

Physical action breaks mental paralysis. We need action.

Pick up your phone. Go to a simple provider website. The first one that comes up. Don't compare. Don't analyze. Don't research more. Just pick one.

Choose the simplest option available. The most basic account. The most straightforward investment. Don't worry about whether it's optimal. Worry about whether it exists. Because right now you have nothing. Simple beats nothing.

Twenty minutes. That's how long this takes. Fill out the application. Answer the questions. Submit it. Done. Account open.

You don't need perfect knowledge. You need movement. Perfect knowledge keeps you paralyzed forever. Movement gets you in the fight. In the fight you can adjust. You can optimize later. But first you have to be in the fight.

The difference between something and nothing is infinite. The difference between optimal and suboptimal is marginal. Get something started. Optimize as you go.

WHAT'S NEXT

Logging in and seeing that number—the one that's a fraction of what it needs to be—that's one of the harder moments in this process. It's not like the situation is hopeless, but because it requires looking at something you've been avoiding, most won't do it. The avoidance is understandable. But avoiding the facts won't solve anything.

The math on retirement changes dramatically depending on when you start and how consistently you contribute. It's not linear. The accounts that are embarrassingly small at 47 look very different at 57 if the contributions become automatic and untouched. Time is the one input you can't recover once it's gone. Time is far more important than money, but you need money to buy back your time. And isn't that the aim? Free time and spare money – simultaneously? Well that's the plan and we are heading there.

The retirement account is now in the system. Contributions running. The long fight engaged. That's position building—slow, invisible, compounding in the background while you handle the present battles.

But there's a problem that building position doesn't solve on its own.

Position takes time to build. Crises don't wait for you to finish building it.

The gap between where you are right now and where you need to be is real. And in that gap lives the most dangerous version of your financial life—the one where everything you've worked for gets erased in a single morning because there was nothing between you and the event that caused it.

You've been one crisis from disaster for longer than you've admitted to yourself. The next chapter is about what that actually means—what it looks like when the crisis arrives before the position is ready—and more importantly, what you do right now, before it does.

CHAPTER 7
ONE-CRISIS-FROM-DISASTER

"There is no more dangerous illusion than the fancies by which people try to avoid illusion." - François de La Rochefoucauld

Monday morning. 9:47 AM.

Your manager calls you into the conference room. HR is already sitting there. You know what this is before anyone says a word.

Unexpected layoff. Budget cuts. Nothing personal. Two weeks severance.

You walk to your car in a daze. Sit in the parking lot. Check your bank account on your phone. The balance barely covers one week of expenses. Maybe less.

No emergency fund. Never built one. Always meant to. Never got around to it. Always something else.

Bills are due in eight days. Rent in twelve. Car payment in fifteen. Insurance after that. The two weeks severance will cover maybe three weeks of expenses if you stretch it. Then nothing.

You run the calculations. Three weeks until complete collapse. Maybe four if you can delay something. Maybe less if anything unexpected happens.

One crisis. One layoff. One unexpected event. Everything worked for has been destroyed, and laid to waste.

You're not the first person this has happened to. You won't be the last. The story is common enough to be predictable. What happens next depends entirely on what you do in the next seventy—two hours.

Most people choose wrong. They panic. They freeze. They make the crisis worse. Then they wait for rock bottom to force change they should have chosen from strength.

THE ROCK BOTTOM LOOP

This is the pattern that destroys people. Here's how it works. Crisis hits. You're forced to change. Not because you want to. Because you have to. Survival demands it. You cut expenses. You hustle. You scrape together money however you can. You do whatever it takes to avoid complete collapse.

And it works. For a while. You stabilize. The immediate crisis passes. You're breathing again. The pressure releases.

That's when the loop tightens.

Pressure releases. Old patterns return. You tell yourself you earned it. You've been suffering. You've been sacrificing. You deserve to relax a little. Spend a little. Live a little. Just until you're fully recovered.

So you revert. Small at first. Maybe a subscription you cancelled. Maybe eating out again. Maybe buying something you've been wanting. Small stuff. Harmless stuff.

Except it's not harmless. Because small reversions become bigger reversions. One month becomes two. Two becomes three. Before you know it you're right back where you were before the crisis. Same spending patterns. Same lack of buffer. Same fragile grip.

Then another crisis hits. Bigger this time. Because you're older. Because your responsibilities have grown. Because life doesn't get easier.

Crisis forces change again. You scramble again. You stabilize again. Pressure releases again. Old patterns return again. The loop repeats.

Each cycle gets harder. Each crisis gets bigger. Each recovery gets shorter. Each reverting gets faster. The loop tightens like a noose until eventually it doesn't release anymore.

That's rock bottom. Complete collapse. Bankruptcy. Eviction. Repossession. All gone. No more cycling. No more recovering. Just devastation.

This is identical to addiction recovery patterns. The addict hits bottom. Gets clean. Does well for a while. Then relapses. Back to using. Eventually another bottom. Worse than before. Another attempt at recovery. Another relapse. Each bottom worse than the last. Each recovery shorter. Until the final bottom that doesn't bounce.

Financial collapse follows the same pattern. Same loop. Same tightening. Same inevitable destruction if you don't break it.

The only way to break the loop is to not revert when pressure releases. To keep executing what works, the very plan that saved you even after the crisis passes. To commit to complete change instead of temporary adjustment.

Most people can't do it. They change when forced. They revert when allowed. They ride the loop all the way to rock bottom. Then they look back and wonder how it got so bad. The loop got so bad. One cycle at a time.

YOU CAN LEAD A HORSE TO WATER

There's an old saying: You can lead a horse to water but you can't make it drink.

The horse dies of thirst within sight of water. Not because water isn't available. Because it refuses to drink. Because drinking requires effort. Because the horse wants rescue, not responsibility.

You're standing at the water right now. This book. These guidelines. These specific actions. The water is here. It's available. It will save you if you drink it.

But I can't make you drink.

You have two choices. Drink now with dignity. Take the red pill. Know the truth and face it. Realize the plan completely. Build your foundation from strength before crisis forces you.

Or wait. Keep doing what you're doing. Stay fragile. Stay vulnerable. Stay one crisis away from collapse. Then when that crisis hits—and it will hit—crawl to the water half—dead and desperate. Drink from devastation instead of choice.

Both versions eventually change. Both versions eventually make the necessary moves. The only difference is timing and position.

Change now from strength. Build your buffer before you need it. Secure your footing before crisis tests it. Employ your strategy and move while you still have options.

Or change later from weakness. After the layoff. After the medical emergency. After the disaster that destroys all the work and effort. It is a lot tougher fighting from your back with gravity working against you.

The water is here. The question is whether you'll drink it now or later. Whether you'll choose change or wait for it to choose you.

I know what you'll choose. Everyone chooses eventually. They drink the water when the thirst becomes unbearable. I'm asking you to be different. Drink before the thirst kills you.

PATH A VS PATH B

So let's break out both paths in full. Complete timelines. Complete outcomes. Then you choose.

Path A: You choose change now. Today. This minute. You carry out every procedure in this book completely. You close the gap. You build the buffer. You attack the debt. You secure retirement. You break the isolation. You execute for forty—two months without reverting. You build unbreakable position.

To make it easier let's start by breaking the schedule down into smaller chunks. Month one: Gap closed. You're living on less than you make for the first time. Uncomfortable but sustainable. Small buffer started. Debt attack beginning. You're in the fight.

Month three: Buffer covers one week of expenses. First small debt eliminated. System running automatically. You're proving to yourself this works.

Month six: Buffer covers two weeks. Second debt eliminated. Monthly attack power growing. Momentum building. You can see progress now.

Year one: Buffer covers one month. Multiple debts eliminated. Retirement contributions started. Position substantially stronger than twelve months ago. Minor crisis hits—car breaks down. Buffer covers it. No panic. No crisis. Just handle it and keep executing.

Year two: Buffer covers three months. Half your consumer debt gone. Retirement growing steadily. Major crisis hits—temporary income loss. Buffer covers it for months. You find new work before buffer depletes. Crisis survived without devastation. Position holds.

Year three: Buffer fully funded. Most debt eliminated. Substantial retirement contributions. Income increases redirected to debt and retirement instead of lifestyle. You're unbreakable now. Crises can't touch you.

Forty—two months: All consumer debt eliminated. Full emergency fund. Strong retirement contributions. Unshakable position. Crisis hits

—doesn't matter what crisis. You handle it from strength. No devastation. No panic. Just enact and continue.

That's Path A. Forty—two months of consistent action from strength. Uncomfortable but sustainable. Disciplined but doable. You built complete security one month at a time.

Now Path B: You don't choose change. You close this book feeling good. You intend to start Monday. Monday comes—you don't start. Something came up. Next week maybe. Next week—still don't start. The book sits on the shelf. Old patterns continue.

Six months pass. Position slightly worse than today. Not dramatically worse. Just slightly. Couple more debts. Buffer still at zero. Gap still unclosed. Still fragile. Still one crisis away from collapse.

Twelve months pass. Positions worsen. More debt accumulated. Still no buffer. Gap wider. You're working harder and falling behind faster. Sometimes you think about that book. Get the plan running. But later. Always later.

Eighteen months: Crisis hits. Not catastrophic. Just medium—sized crisis. Car needs major repair. Appliance breaks. Medical issue. Something that wouldn't destroy someone with a buffer. But you have no buffer. Credit cards cover it. Debt grows. Position deteriorates further.

Twenty—four months: Position critical. Debt substantial. Buffer still zero. Gap massive. You're barely keeping lights on. Then the real crisis hits. Layoff. Medical emergency. Disaster. Something big.

Complete collapse. Can't cover rent. Can't make payments. Eviction notice. Repossession. The entirety falling apart simultaneously. This is rock bottom. This is where the loop ends when you don't break it.

If you're reading this before that moment, you still have choices. Path A is still open. The fact that you're here means it's not too late.

Only now—broken, desperate, destroyed—do you commit. Only now do you follow the blueprint. Only now do you change completely. Same procedures you could have acted two years ago from strength. But now you're executing from devastation.

Rebuilding from rock bottom takes longer. Costs more. Hurts worse. You're starting from below zero. Climbing out of a hole before you can even get to ground level. Years of performance just to get back to where you started.

But people do it. Every day, people climb back from exactly this and further. the SOP works from wherever you start—even here.

That's Path B. Two years of delay. Two years of deterioration. Complete collapse. Then the same commitment you could have made from strength, now made from wreckage.

Path A is still available. Right now. Today. The gap between the two paths closes the moment you choose—and you can choose this minute.

Both paths conclude eventually. Both commit completely eventually. Both change entirely eventually. The only difference is timing and position.

Path A changes now by choice from strength. Path B changes later by force from devastation.

There is no Path C. There is no middle ground where you *kind of* commit and *kind of* change and somehow avoid both hard effort and eventual collapse. That path doesn't exist. It's an illusion. A fantasy. A lie you tell yourself to avoid choosing.

Path A or Path B. Choose now or choose later. Strength or devastation. Those are your options.

Inaction isn't neutrality. Inaction is choosing Path B by default. Every day you delay is another day down Path B. Every day closer to the collapse that makes the choice for you. Choose consciously. Right now.

Which means action isn't just possible—it's the one thing that actually changes the math. And action starts small. Smaller than you think.

THE COLLAPSE TIMELINE

Watch carefully as Path B unfolds. Week by week. So you know what you're choosing if you choose delay.

Crisis hits. Let's say layoff since that's the opening scenario. You have two weeks severance and almost nothing saved. The clock starts.

Week one: Shock. Denial. You tell yourself you'll find something fast. You've always landed on your feet before. You'll be fine. You apply to a few jobs. Not many. Not aggressively. Just enough to feel like you're doing something.

Week two: Severance runs out. No job yet. You're dipping into the small amount you had saved. Bills are due. You pay some. Delay others. Hope something comes through soon.

Week three: Savings gone. No job. Rent due. Can't pay it. You borrow from family. From friends. Anyone who will lend. You promise to pay it back soon. Next paycheck for sure. They lend it. You pay rent. Crisis delayed one month.

Week four: Still no job. More bills due. Credit cards cover some. Can't cover all. Start getting late notices. Start ignoring calls from creditors. Too ashamed to answer. Too overwhelmed to deal with it.

This is the scenario the buffer is built to prevent. Building it now—even small, even slowly—changes this entire chain of events.

Week six: Credit cards maxed. Can't borrow more. Family tapped out. Friends avoiding your calls. Rent due again. Can't pay it. Eviction notice posted. Thirty days to vacate.

Week eight: Car payment missed twice. Repossession warning. No car means no way to get to interviews. No way to work if you find something. Position deteriorating exponentially now.

Week ten: Evicted. Living with family if they'll take you. Or friends. Or in your car if you still have it. Or in a shelter. Rock bottom. Complete collapse. All that you feared would happen, happened.

That's ten weeks from crisis to complete collapse when you have no buffer and don't activate the game-plan immediately. Ten weeks from employed to homeless. Ten weeks from paycheck to devastation.

And it's eight weeks to recovery with the right moves activated immediately. The same ten weeks. Completely different outcome. That difference is why this system exists.

Now the alternative timeline. Same crisis. Same layoff. But this time you have a buffer and you act immediately.

Week one: Crisis hits. You're ready. You have three months of expenses saved. You're not panicking. You immediately cut expenses to minimum. Cancel anything non—essential. Apply aggressively for every relevant position. Execute the job search like a military campaign.

Week two: Buffer covering expenses. Multiple applications daily. Networking aggressively. Using every contact. Treating this like the fight it is.

Week four: First interviews. Buffer still stable. Position still strong. You're selective about opportunities. You can afford to be because you're not desperate. You negotiate from strength.

Week eight: Job secured. Better than the last one. You learned from the crisis. You negotiated harder because you weren't desperate. Buffer still intact. You keep living lean. Rebuild what you used. Increase the buffer. Never get caught vulnerable again.

Same crisis. Completely different outcomes. The difference? The buffer. The strategy you employed. The position you built before crisis tested you.

That's what you're choosing between. Collapse in ten weeks or recovery in eight. Devastation or resilience. Path B or Path A. The crisis doesn't care which path you chose. But the outcome depends entirely on it.

NO RASH DECISIONS

There's a difference between rash and urgent. Most people confuse them. So let me clarify.

Rash is unsustainable desperation. It is frantic and chaotic. It is exhausting. We will not operate from this state.

Urgent is calculated sustainable action executed immediately. It is based on controlled and determined energy. Urgent is what a highly paid respected professional employs when immediacy is the order of the day.

Strategic doesn't mean slow. Strategic means the right decision delivered immediately. The decision that works. The approach that's sustainable. The SOP that can function for the full duration required.

Every day you delay is another day of interest compounding against you. Another day closer to crisis. Another day of capacity wasted. Another day that could have been building position instead of maintaining fragility.

The urgency is real. The timeline is real. The consequences of delay are real. But the effort is strategic. Sustainable intensity over sustainable timeline to sustainable outcome.

Don't be rash. Be urgent. Start now. do this right. Sustain completely. Win decisively.

IN ONE PLACE

You've read the whole book now. Every chapter. Every aspect. Every principle. We are going to put it all in one place so you can see the complete system.

The enemy: Paralysis. Not money. Not circumstances. Paralysis. The frozen decision—making that keeps you trapped in analysis instead of action. The OODA loop that never completes. The endless calculating that produces no movement.

The solution: Faster OODA loops. Observe the situation clearly. Orient yourself to reality without delusion. Decide on the next move. Act immediately. Then loop again. Faster cycles. Faster decisions. Faster movement. That's how you beat paralysis.

The framework: This minute. This week. This month. Break every overwhelming problem into immediate action, short—term execution, and medium—term system. Always three timelines. Always specific actions. Always completable steps.

The principles from combat that apply to money: Shu Ha Ri—follow the form until you master it, then adapt it to yourself. Tactical breath —when paralyzed, breathe and move. OODA loops—decide and act faster than the problem evolves. Economy of motion—every action serves the goal, nothing wasted. The long fight—sustainable systems beat heroic effort over decades. Your fight—fight on your terms, not on the fight others want you to fight. The austere path—simple living creates freedom. Every move serves the goal—no wasted effort, no wasted resources. Training partners—you can't do this alone. Mentorship—glue yourself to someone who's won the fight you're fighting.

The sequence: Close the gap. Build the buffer. Attack debt. Build resilience. Secure retirement. Maintain forever. Each stage builds on the previous. Each stage creates capacity for the next. Actualize in order. Complete each stage. Never revert.

The timeline: Forty—two months of full commitment without reverting. That's three and a half years of systematic discipline. That's what it takes to go from fragile to unbreakable. Shorter timelines produce incomplete results. Longer timelines lose momentum. Forty—two months is the fight.

The commitment: No reverting when pressure releases. This is where most people fail. Crisis forces change. Pressure releases. They celebrate by reverting. The loop tightens. Don't revert. Produce through the full agenda. Maintain discipline after the crisis passes. That's how you break the loop.

That's the complete system. Simple enough to understand. Hard enough to require your maximum effort and all you have to give. Effective enough to produce complete security if you do it properly. The question is whether you'll use it.

THE FINAL TRUTH

Money won't fix your broken system.

That's the truth you need to accept right now. If I handed you enough money to pay off all your debt today, you'd be back in debt within two years. Maybe less. Because the SOP that created the debt is still running.

If I gave you a massive raise, your lifestyle would expand to consume it within months. The gap would remain. The fragility would persist. Nothing would fundamentally change. Because the SOP is broken.

You need a new system. Not perfect timing. A new system that functions regardless of circumstances. That happens regardless of motivation. That sustains regardless of difficulty.

The SOP I've given you works. It's been proven by thousands of people who started from worse positions than you and built complete security. It works if you work it.

But—and this is critical—the SOP only works if you work it. Knowing the SOP changes nothing. Understanding the plan changes nothing. Agreeing with the principles changes nothing. Only action changes will change your course.

You know all you need to know now. The only question remaining is whether you'll deliver on what you know. Answer that question with action. Right now.

YOUR NEXT MOVE

Close this book. Take a tactical breath. Run an OODA loop. Decide your next move. Act.

One move this minute.

Cancel a subscription. Write down an expense to cut. Make a call about a bill. List something to sell. Text one person to break the isolation. One move. Ten minutes maximum.

Do it before you set this book down. Because the moment you set this book down without taking action is the moment the old system reclaims you. The moment paralysis wins. The moment you choose Path B by default.

Tomorrow another move. Day after that another. Next week seven moves. Next month thirty moves. One thousand two hundred sixty small moves over forty—two months equals a completely different position.

The first move is the hardest. The first move breaks the paralysis. The first move proves to yourself that you can do this. Make the first move right now. Then the second move becomes easier. Then the third. Then momentum carries you.

THE WARRIOR'S PATH

Miyamoto Musashi said the ultimate aim of martial arts is not having to use them.

You train so hard that nobody challenges you. You build such a strong position that threats don't materialize. You become so dangerous that conflicts resolve before they escalate.

Same principle applies here. Execute for forty—two months. Secure your foundation. Maintain your discipline. The crisis plan becomes unnecessary because you're no longer in crisis.

The buffer protects you. The discipline sustains you. The position elevates you. Crises still happen but they don't destroy you. They're inconveniences, not catastrophes. Problems to solve, not disasters to survive.

That's what forty—two months of commitment produces. A position so strong that the fight changes. The enemy was crisis. The enemy was fragility. do this right and those enemies can't touch you anymore.

But understand something clearly: You are at war.

You're at war with a system that wants to consume you. A system that profits from your debt. That benefits from your desperation. That needs you fragile and dependent and trapped.

They win when you're paralyzed. When you're drowning. When you're isolated. When you're making minimum payments forever. When you're working until you collapse. When you're too broken to fight back.

You are not paralyzed. You are reading. You are building the plan. That is the opposite of paralyzed—that is someone who decided to fight back.

You win when you move. When you perform. When you fight with support. When you pay off debt completely. When you build unbreakable position. When you secure your freedom.

Act like you're at war. Because you are. Fight like the warrior you're capable of becoming. Because that's what this requires. Win like your family's future depends on it. Because it does.

THE CALL

Blunt truth time. No softening it. No making it easier to hear.

You're at the bottom of a hole. Nobody's coming to rescue you. Nobody's going to do this for you. Nobody's going to make it easier or give you special conditions or wait for you to be ready.

You climb out or you stay in.

Climbing requires one thing: Willingness to suffer now to avoid suffering later.

The next forty—two months are going to be hard. Really hard. Austere living while everyone around you is consuming. Saying no to things you want. Being judged for your choices. Watching others take vacations while you attack debt. Missing out while you build stability. Sacrificing while others indulge.

It's going to hurt. Every day for forty—two months it's going to hurt. You're going to want to quit. You're going to want to revert. You're going to want to take a break. You're going to tell yourself you've earned it. You deserve it. Just this once.

That's the moment you either win or lose this fight. That moment of temptation. That moment of weakness. That moment when reverting feels justified.

Push through it or quit. Those are your options. And if you quit, everything you built collapses. All the sacrifice wasted. All the progress lost. Back to the loop. Back to fragility. Back to the hole.

You haven't quit yet. You're still here. That's not a small thing—that's the characteristic that separates people who come through this from people who don't.

So yes, it's going to hurt. Yes, it's going to be hard. Yes, you're going to suffer for forty—two months.

But the alternatives hurt more.

Working until you physically die hurts more. Getting laid off and losing it all hurts more. Teaching your kids to drown in the same debt that's drowning you hurts more. Carrying this weight alone for decades hurts more. Living one crisis from disaster forever hurts more. Hitting rock bottom after years of denial hurts more.

You are fighting to prevent that. Every step in this system is a step away from that outcome. That is worth something. That is worth a lot.

Choose your pain. Discipline now or regret later. Sacrifice now or devastation later. Implementation now or collapse later.

You've already shown you can handle hard. You're handling hard right now. The question is just which kind of hard—and this kind builds something real on the other side.

I can't make this easier for you. I can only tell you it's worth it. Forty—two months of hard commitment produces freedom nothing else can buy. Choose the hard now. Choose the discipline. Choose the warrior's path.

THE COMMITMENT

Say it. Out loud if you can. In your head if you must. But say it and mean it.

"I will enact these strategies for thirty days without reverting. I will close the gap. I will not make excuses. I will not delay. I will not halfway commit. I will follow through completely."

"When the gap is closed, I will move to the next objective the same way. Buffer. Then debt. Then retirement. Then maintenance."

"I will do this for forty—two months. I will not quit. I will not revert. I will not celebrate progress by reverting to old patterns. I will secure my position completely."

"I commit completely. Starting this minute."

If you say those words, prove them with action this minute. Right now. Before you move on to the next sentence. One action. Cancel something. Write something. Call someone. Move.

THE FIRE

There's a fire that burns in some men. A refusal to accept defeat. A refusal to quit. A refusal to surrender to circumstances or systems or expectations.

That fire is either in you or it's not. I can't create it. I can only pour gasoline on it if it exists.

Maybe the fire has been buried. Buried under years of defeat. Under years of trying and failing. Under years of being told you can't. Under years of evidence that you won't.

This book poured gasoline on that buried fire. Every chapter. Every method. Every combat principle. Every blunt truth. Gasoline on the fire.

The fire is burning right now. You can feel it. That anger at your situation. That refusal to stay where you are. That determination to be different. That commitment to fight. The fire is burning.

Question is: Will you let it burn? Will you feed it with action? Will you let it consume the old system and forge you into something stronger?

Or will you smother it with excuses? With delay? With justifications? With comfort? With the same patterns that got you here?

Feed the fire. Let it burn. Let it forge you. Move.

TRUTH ABOUT MOTIVATION

You're motivated right now. Fired up. Ready to execute. You're going to start Monday. You're going to commit completely. You're going to do this.

Monday comes. Motivation's gone. Don't feel like it anymore. The urgency has faded. Maybe Wednesday. Wednesday comes. Still don't feel motivated. Maybe next week. Next week comes. Same thing. Motivation is gone and isn't coming back.

Here's the truth about motivation that nobody wants to hear: Motivation is garbage.

Motivation doesn't create action. Action creates motivation.

You don't wait to feel motivated and then move. You move and then motivation follows. The first move feels impossible. Do it anyway. Movement creates motivation—not the other way around. Start before you're ready, because ready is a lie.

Second move is slightly easier. Third move easier still. By the tenth move you're not relying on motivation anymore. You're relying on momentum. Momentum carries you when motivation fails. And motivation always fails.

The SOP I've given you doesn't require motivation. It requires movement. First move creates second move. Second creates third. Momentum compounds. System runs automatically.

Don't wait to feel motivated. You'll never feel motivated. Move anyway. Action creates motivation. Momentum sustains motion. First move is all that matters. Make it now.

NEXT 10 MINUTES

Close this book. You have one decision to make right now, and it's super simple.

Do one thing. Ten minutes maximum. Cancel a subscription. Write down an expense to cut. Call about a bill. List something to sell. Text one person so you're no longer carrying this alone. One thing—that's it.

Not because one thing solves the problem. It doesn't. But because the person who puts this book down and does nothing will pick it up again in six months from a worse place. That's not a threat—it's just the math of inaction. The gap doesn't pause while you decide. The debt doesn't wait for a better Monday.

The person who does one thing tonight does another thing tomorrow. And another. That's how this actually works—not through a single moment of transformation, but through small moves that compound until one day the math is finally on your side.

You already know which version of this story you want. The only question is whether you start writing it right now or hand that decision to circumstances instead.

One thing. Put the book down and go do it.

BATTLE CONTINUES

The same layoff. The same Monday morning, the same conference room, the same drive home. Two completely different outcomes determined entirely by what was or wasn't built before that morning.

Ten weeks is not long. It is not enough time to improvise your way out of a position you spent years building up to. But eight weeks is enough time to find the next thing if you go in prepared. That's the entire argument for everything in this book compressed into one scenario: the crisis doesn't care whether you're ready. The outcome does.

The man with the buffer survives the layoff. The man without it doesn't. That's the whole argument.

But there's a weight that runs parallel to all of this. A weight that has nothing to do with bank balances or debt payoff timelines or runway calculations.

It's the weight of watching. Of comparison. Of standing in the stands at your daughter's game next to a man who just wrote a check for travel fees you couldn't cover. Of saying *maybe next year* when you know next year isn't guaranteed either.

The financial fight is tactical. Measurable. There are numbers to track and sequences to follow and positions to secure. You're learning to win that fight.

The next chapter is about the other one—the one you carry in silence.

SOP: THIS MINUTE

Calculate your runway.

Not an estimate. The actual number.

If your income stopped today—right now, this minute—how many days until you can't cover your obligations? Open your bank account. Look at the current balance. Open your bills. Add up what's due in the next thirty days. Divide your balance by your daily burn rate.

Write that number down.

_____ days.

That number is your fragility score. That number is the distance between where you are right now and the scenario that opened this chapter. If that number is less than thirty, you are one event from disaster. If it's less than fourteen, the crisis is already almost here—you just haven't met it yet.

Don't look away from it. The man who looks away from that number is the man in the parking lot. The man who looks directly at it and decides to act is the man who never sees that parking lot.

You've calculated it. Now you know exactly what you're fighting against. That's the first move.

SOP: THIS WEEK

Identify your three fragility points.

Every man in the one-crisis-from-disaster position has specific vulnerabilities.

Monday: Write down the single event most likely to destroy your current position. Not the scariest event. The most likely one. Job loss.

Medical bill. Car failure. Relationship disruption. Be honest. What's the one thing that, if it happened tomorrow, collapses everything?

That is your Primary Fragility Point. Write it down by name.

Tuesday: Write down your second and third most likely threats. Same exercise. Same honesty. No minimizing. No "it probably won't happen." You're doing threat assessment, not wishful thinking.

Wednesday: For each threat, answer one question: *How many days of buffer would neutralize this threat?* Not eliminate it. Neutralize it—give you enough runway to respond from strength instead of panic.

A thirty-day buffer neutralizes most job loss scenarios. A sixty-day buffer handles most medical emergencies before insurance processes. A ninety-day buffer makes you nearly untouchable by the crises that destroy most men.

Write down the buffer target that neutralizes each threat.

Thursday: Look at where you currently are in the chapter sequence. Have you closed the gap (Chapter 4)? Have you started the buffer (Chapter 3)? If you've been skipping ahead, stop. Go back. The sequence is the sequence for a reason. You cannot build defensive depth from a leaking position.

Friday: Write down one specific action—not a category, a specific action—that moves you one step closer to your buffer target. Cancel the subscription. Pick up the extra shift. List the item to sell. One action with a name and a deadline.

Saturday and Sunday: Execute the Friday action. Not plan to. Execute.

SOP: THIS MONTH

Close your first fragility point.

Week one: Your Primary Fragility Point is identified. Now you build toward neutralizing it using the same three sources from Chapter 3: cut the waste, sell the unused, generate additional income. All buffer-building proceeds from those three levers. You already know how to work them. Work them toward this specific target.

Week two: Review your runway number from this minute's SOP. Calculate it again. Has it improved? Even one day of improvement is movement. Movement is the difference between Path A and Path B. Document the change. You're building evidence that the system works —evidence you'll need in month seven when motivation is long gone and only proof keeps you moving.

Week three: Identify whether your fragility point is structural or behavioral. A structural fragility point—income too low, single income stream, no marketable skills—requires a different response than a behavioral one—spending that eliminates buffer as fast as it's built, reverting under pressure, making emotional purchases after stressful weeks. Most men have both. Knowing which is which determines what the fix looks like.

Week four: Calculate total buffer built this month. Whatever the number is, it's more than last month. More than the parking lot version of you had. Every day of runway you add is a day of distance between you and rock bottom. The loop can't tighten what it can't reach.

You don't have to be fully defended by the end of this month. You have to be less fragile than you were at the start of it. That's the objective. Less fragile. More runway. One crisis further from disaster.

That's how you break the loop. Not in a single heroic moment. One month at a time, until the crises that used to destroy you become inconveniences you handle before lunch.

STANDARD OPERATING SYSTEM

This chapter is different from the others. Every other chapter targets a specific battle—the gap, the debt, the retirement account. This chapter targets the pattern beneath all of them. The loop that undoes every battle you win the moment pressure releases.

The SOP here isn't about money. It's about not reverting.

You've been building position across every previous chapter. The gap is closing or closed. The buffer is growing. The debt is under attack. All of that is now a structure worth defending.

Your job this month is to defend it. Defend it from yourself. From the part of you that wants to breathe out when things ease up. From the reversion instinct that has broken every previous attempt. The toughest enemy you will ever face is yourself.

Execute the SOP. Stay in the sequence. Don't revert.

Forty-two months. Not forty-two *perfect* months. Forty-two months of not quitting.

CHAPTER 8
FIRST RESOURCE

"Between stimulus and response, there is a space. In that space is our power to choose." — Viktor Frankl

You are already behind before your alarm goes off.

You know this because the first thing you do, before your feet hit the floor, is calculate. How much is in the account. What's due this week. Whether the number in your head matches the number that's actually there. You run the math in the dark, alone, before anyone in the house is awake, because at some level you know that if you stop running it, something will fall.

That calculation loop — the one that never fully closes — is not a discipline problem. It's not a motivation problem. It's a resource allocation problem, and the resource being consumed isn't money.

It's attention.

When a man is fighting for basic footing — roof, food, the lights staying on — his mind operates in a mode that evolution designed for immediate survival. Threat detection. Risk avoidance. Minimum necessary output to keep the danger from arriving. That mode is efficient for what it was designed for. It is catastrophic for what you actually need to do now.

You cannot think strategically from inside survival mode. You cannot see opportunity from the bottom of a hole. You cannot identify your assets when all of your cognitive resources are allocated to not losing what you have.

This is not weakness. This is how brains work. A man drowning doesn't assess the quality of the water.

ABOVE THE LINE

Abraham Maslow mapped this decades ago. His hierarchy of needs describes a pyramid where the lower levels must be secured before the upper levels become accessible. Physiological needs first — food, water, shelter, sleep. Safety next — financial security, predictable environment, protection from loss. Only once those two floors are stable does the mind naturally begin to reach upward. Belonging. Esteem. Self-actualization.

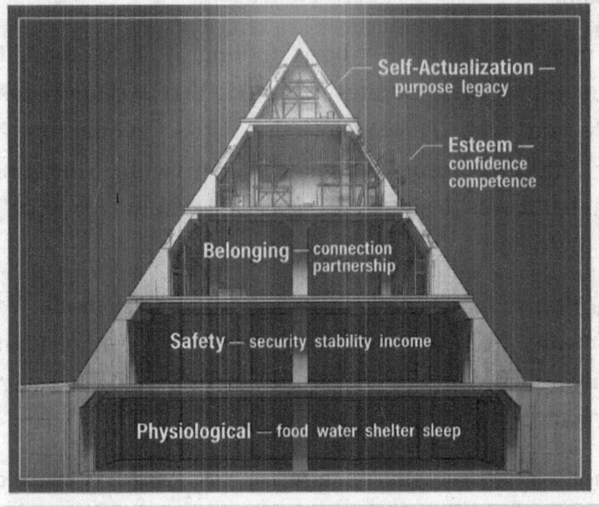

The man in the calculation loop is living on the first floor. Sometimes the second. His mind is not deficient. His mind is doing exactly what a mind does when the lower floors are unsecured — it allocates everything to securing them, because from an evolutionary standpoint, that is the only rational response to the situation.

The problem is that income growth, opportunity identification, and strategic planning all happen above the first floor. They require the cognitive and creative capacity that survival mode specifically suppresses.

This is why financial advice that tells a man to "think bigger" while he's drowning is not just unhelpful — it's insulting. You cannot think bigger from inside a narrowed survival state. The bandwidth isn't available. It's already committed.

The path forward is not about thinking differently. It's about buying back the bandwidth. Creating enough stability on the lower floors that the upper floors become accessible again. Not fully secured — that takes years. But stable enough. Stable enough that the calculation loop quiets from a roar to a background hum. Stable enough that you can look up from the hole and see the edge.

That margin is what you're building. That is what the $500 buffer is actually doing. That is what closing the monthly gap is actually doing. Not just arithmetic improvement. Cognitive reclamation. Buying back the mental space that survival mode has been consuming.

The moment you feel that space begin to open — and you will feel it, it's unmistakable — something important needs to happen. You need to stop and use it before the reflex to fill it takes over.

THE PAUSE

In martial arts, every serious practitioner learns this: between what hits you and what you do next, there is a space. The untrained person collapses it. Insult arrives, anger erupts, action fires — one automatic chain. The trained fighter learns to expand it. To feel the pressure rising and hold the space open long enough to choose.

That gap — that brief opening where deliberate response replaces automatic reaction — is where everything real happens. It's where leaders lead and followers follow. Where the person who makes the call differs from the person who freezes.

Financial survival mode collapses that space entirely. Not metaphorically — literally. When the first-floor threats are active, the brain's threat-response architecture compresses decision windows. You react. You manage the immediate. You handle what's in front of you. The pause disappears because the system perceives that there's no time for it.

Creating margin — financial breathing room — doesn't just give you more money. It gives you back the pause. The space between threat and response. The moment where you can see clearly instead of react automatically.

The pause is not passive. It is not rest. It is active reconnaissance. It is the moment where, instead of running your survival calculations, you run a different kind of math. Not what's due this week. What you're actually capable of. Not what's depleting you. What you could build.

A man with no breathing room cannot take the pause. He is constantly in the stimulus-response chain, every demand pulling an immediate reaction, every month a new version of the same fire.

A man with $500 in a buffer account, a closing gap, and two fewer crisis events per quarter begins to have the pause available. Not frequently. Not yet. But occasionally. Long enough to look up. Long enough to see the edge of the hole.

That is when the second fight begins.

CARDS YOU HOLD

Every man sits down to a different hand.

Your income, your obligations, your geography, your history, your education, your network, your family structure — these are the cards already dealt. They are not good or bad in themselves. They are the starting position. The terrain you're fighting on.

Some men were dealt high cards in certain suits — a trade learned young, a technical skill developed over a decade, a geography that puts them near a specific kind of demand. Some were dealt low cards in suits they didn't choose — high obligations early, interrupted education, a region with limited opportunity in their field.

You do not get to re-deal. You play from what you hold.

The mistake most men make is one of two opposite errors. The first error is pretending the cards don't matter — that any man can build any income from any starting position through sheer will. That's motivational content for people who don't need motivation. It isn't strategy. The second error is using the cards as a verdict — this hand can't win, so why play. Both errors produce the same outcome: paralysis dressed in different clothes.

Your hand is specific. Your path forward is built from that specificity, not despite it.

The man who spent fifteen years in the trades holds cards that a college-educated office worker doesn't. The office worker holds cards the trades man doesn't. Neither hand is better. But they play differently. The trade man's income offense looks different from the office worker's. The man with a young family plays different than the man alone. The man in a rural area plays different from the man in a major city.

This is not a limitation. It's your map. You cannot navigate by someone else's map. You need yours.

When the pause becomes available — when you have enough breathing room to stop running the survival calculations and actually think — the first question is not how do I make more money. It is: what cards am I actually holding?

Not what you wish you had. Not what your neighbor was dealt. What is actually in your hand, right now. Skills accumulated over years. Knowledge that feels obvious to you but isn't to others. Problems you've solved that other people are still stuck on. Access you have that people will pay to navigate. Resources that are underutilized. Capabilities you've been giving away for free.

That inventory is your reconnaissance report. You cannot build an income strategy from wishes. You build it from what's real and already present.

BREATHING ROOM

The reason creative problem-solving requires space isn't philosophical. It's neurological.

The prefrontal cortex — the part of the brain responsible for long-range planning, pattern recognition across time, creative synthesis — is suppressed by the stress hormones that flood the system under sustained threat. Cortisol, the primary stress hormone, directly inhibits the cognitive functions you need for strategic thinking. This is not a deficiency of will. It is a biological mechanism. The threatened animal focuses on the immediate threat. The calm animal can survey the terrain.

The breathing room you're building does something most financial books don't account for: it changes what you can see. Not because the opportunities weren't there before. Because your threat-narrowed attention couldn't reach them.

Men describe this consistently when they cross the threshold — when the buffer is built, the gap is closing, the calculation loop quiets enough to sleep through. They say: I started noticing things. Conversations that had something in them. Problems people mentioned that I already knew how to solve. Patterns I'd seen for years that suddenly looked like a path.

The opportunities weren't new. The perception was.

This is why the sequence matters. Buffer first. Gap closed second. Then — and only then — can the income offense have the foundation it requires. Not because of money. Because of cognitive reclamation. Because you need access to the upper floors of the pyramid before you can build anything on them.

The income offensive built from survival mode is built from desperation, and desperation-built income streams smell like desperation to the people you're trying to serve. They collapse under the first real obstacle because the foundation is emotional, not strategic.

The income offensive built from the pause — from genuine assessment of your actual cards, your actual capabilities, your actual market — is built from clarity. That holds.

RECONNAISSANCE MISSION

Before any income strategy, a reconnaissance mission. On yourself.

The pause gives you the capacity for it. The buffer gives you the time. The closed gap gives you the attention that isn't already committed to crisis management.

Three questions. Answer them in a physical notebook, not your phone. Writing forces the kind of processing that reading and thinking alone don't produce. It slows you down enough for accuracy.

Question one: What problems do I already know how to solve that other people are still stuck on?

Not what you wish you could do. What you've actually figured out. The thing that feels obvious to you now because you did it the hard way. The knowledge that took years to acquire that you now give away in ten-minute conversations. Whatever someone calls you about at ten at night because you're the person they know who knows this particular thing.

That ten-at-night call is market-validated data. People don't pay money casually, but they spend trust and time even more reluctantly. If they're spending that on you for this, someone else is charging for it. You've been doing the work. You haven't been capturing the value.

Before that question can be answered honestly, one earlier question needs clearing first. Most men skip it because it sounds soft. It isn't.

What did you do between the ages of eight and twelve, before anyone told you it wasn't practical?

Before the job requirements. Before the family obligations. Before the part of your brain that filters everything through whether it pays. What did you do in the hours that were fully yours?

Write it down. Write fast. Don't edit the first answer — the first answer is almost always the most honest one.

Then: what would you read about on a Sunday morning with no deadline attached? When have you been so absorbed in something that you lost track of time completely? What subject or skill makes you genuinely irritated when someone gets it wrong — not because you're a perfectionist about everything, but because you actually care about this particular thing?

That last one is the most underused diagnostic of the four. Genuine irritation at poor execution is almost always a marker of real competence and deep investment. You don't get angry at mediocrity in things you don't care about. The things that make you stop and say "that's wrong and it matters" are almost always things you know well and could do significantly better. That irritation is pointing at something. Write down what it's pointing at.

These answers don't directly tell you what to build. They tell you what won't feel like punishment in month eight when the novelty is gone and you're still doing it anyway. The man who builds income from something that landed in this list operates differently from the man who builds from calculation alone. He talks about it differently. He attracts different clients. People can feel the difference between a man doing something because he chose it and a man doing something because he's trapped in it.

You've spent enough time in the second category.

Question two: What can I produce that other people would consume?

Not manufacture — produce. A document. A process. Knowledge organized into a format that travels. A demonstration of a skill in a medium that can reach people who can't afford your time directly. The trades man who knows how to diagnose a specific category of electrical problem and can explain it has something. The manager who's developed a system for running difficult conversations and can articulate it has something. The man who's navigated a specific bureaucratic maze and came out the other side has something.

You don't need a large audience. You need the right ten people who need exactly what you know. In most cases that's enough to begin.

Question three: Where does my week have untapped hours?

Be honest. Not theoretical hours — real hours. Hours that exist even in your current schedule, even with your current obligations, that are currently going toward consumption. The algorithm. The scroll. The passive entertainment that you do not choose so much as fall into.

This question is not about grinding more. It is about allocation. You already have hours. They are already being spent. The question is on what, and whether that's the choice you're making intentionally.

Most men who run this honest accounting find ten to fifteen hours per week that are genuinely unallocated — not committed to family, recovery, or meaningful activity, but defaulting to consumption because consumption is frictionless and creation requires activation energy. That is where the early build happens. Not through impossible sacrifice of sleep and family time. Through reclaiming what's already not being used well.

INCOME INVENTORY

The three questions point the direction. This exercise makes it specific.

Open your notebook to a fresh page. Draw four columns.

Column A: Professional Skills. What you do at work that someone else couldn't do without the same training or years of experience. Don't filter for what feels impressive. Write what's accurate.

Column B: Physical Capabilities. What you can build, fix, install, move, train, or maintain with your hands. Trades count here. So does anything developed outside work — the renovation you did yourself, the engines you've rebuilt, the thing you figured out because no one else in your circle knew how.

Column C: Knowledge and Experience. What took years to acquire that other people are still figuring out. Military background. Certifications. Industry knowledge that feels obvious to you and foreign to most people outside it. The maze you navigated — medical, legal, bureaucratic, technical — that you came out the other side of knowing exactly how it works.

Column D: What People Ask You For. This is the most valuable column on the page, and most men underestimate it. Write every example you can recall of someone bringing you a problem because you were the person they knew who knew this particular thing. Recent examples. Old examples. The calls, the texts, the "hey can I pick your brain." All of it.

That fourth column is already market-validated data. These people are not paying you yet. But they are voting with their time and their trust, which is harder to earn than money. Whatever they're bringing to you, someone else charges for it. You have been doing the work and not capturing the value.

Now look for intersections between columns. HVAC experience in Column A plus neighbors asking about their units in Column D equals a diagnostic service. Security background in Column C plus people asking about home protection in Column D equals a consultation business. Logistics expertise in Column A plus small business owners asking how to manage freight in Column D equals a specialized practice.

Two complementary skills narrow the field and raise the price. Website development alone is a commodity. Website development plus HIPAA compliance knowledge is a specialized practice. Drone operation plus photography is an aerial inspection business. The intersection between what you've built and what people are already requesting is where the starting point lives.

Before any idea gets your time, run it through one test: does this make someone's life meaningfully better, easier, or less painful? If yes, it's viable. If no, it fails regardless of how much discipline you apply to it. The product or service is never the point. The value delivered to the buyer is the point.

INCOME OFFENSE

What you're building is not a side hustle in the gig economy sense. You are building an additional income stream from genuine capability and real-world demand.

The difference matters. Gig economy income is fungible labor — your time exchanged for a predetermined rate. You are interchangeable. The platform owns the relationship. You remain dependent on the platform's continued goodwill, algorithm, and policy.

Income built from specific expertise — your actual knowledge, your actual skills, your actual access — is not fungible. You are not interchangeable. You own the relationship. You control the value delivered. Over time, that compounds in ways gig income never does.

The path from zero to first income from a capability-based stream is slower than picking up a second job. This is true. It typically takes three to six months before the first real return, and twelve to eighteen months before it stabilizes. This is also why most men who try it quit — they expect gig-economy speed from expertise-economy work, and when it doesn't arrive, they conclude it doesn't work.

It works. But it runs on a different clock.

The man with a closed gap and a buffer has a different relationship with that timeline than the man who is still in the hole. The man in the hole needs income this week. He doesn't have eighteen months. He should pick up the second job, the extra shift, the gig work — to build the buffer first. The man with the buffer can play the longer game. He doesn't need this particular stream to produce next week. He needs it to produce by month twelve.

That patience is only possible from a stable position. Which is why the sequence is the sequence.

One stream built well. Built from your actual inventory. Producing reliably. Then, and only then, a second stream considered. Not before.

Most men who fail at income building fail because they pursue too many streams before any single stream is producing. The focus fragments. Nothing gets enough attention to compound. They work harder than any single-stream man and produce less. Because they scattered their limited resource — time and attention — across too many incomplete bets.

MARKETING TOOL

Right now, tonight, you're going to open your phone and do what you did last night. Scroll. Watch. Like. Move to the next thing.

Someone's fishing trip. Someone's opinion. A clip from a game. A video that's three minutes long about nothing you needed to know.

Thirty minutes. Maybe an hour. Maybe more, because the algorithm knows exactly what to feed you next.

Add it up. Three hours a week is twelve hours a month. Twelve hours a month is a hundred and forty-four hours a year. Six full days.

Six days you handed to somebody else's growth.

And while you were watching, someone else was filming. Their work. Their skill. Their result. Their next client finding them in a feed on a Tuesday night.

That person and you have the exact same device. The exact same camera. The exact same platform. The only difference is what they pointed it at.

Money lost can be recovered. Time lost is permanent. There is no account you can fund to buy it back. The man who loses five hundred dollars can earn five hundred dollars again. The man who spends three hours watching someone else build something cannot get those three hours back. The only choice available is what he does with the next three hours.

Every skilled trade, every service, every capability you identified in the inventory has a visible result. Something that can be demonstrated in under a minute and put in front of people who need exactly what you offer.

The painter has the transformation. Before the room, after the room. The detailer has the restoration. The woodworker has the build. Each of those is content that proves the skill, shows the result, and reaches a buyer who was already looking for what you offer.

You don't have to become an influencer. You have to point the camera at the work and press record. The man who does that consistently is not competing with other businesses. He is one. He's building a permanent record of his competence and distributing it for free to the exact people who need to see it.

IN SEQUENCE

This is how it works in practice.

Phase one is the position fight — everything in the previous chapters. Buffer built. Gap closed. Survival mode quieted enough that the calculation loop is no longer consuming all available attention. This phase is not glamorous. It is not visible to anyone outside your household. It is the only foundation that works.

Phase two is the reconnaissance — the pause, the notebook, the three questions, the inventory. This phase runs in the space that phase one has created. It cannot run before phase one creates that space. Most men try to skip phase one and go directly to phase two. They pick up a side income idea while still drowning in the gap, and it fails — not because the idea was wrong, but because the foundation wasn't there to hold it.

Phase three is the build — one stream, first principles, the longer clock, enough patience to let it compound. This phase begins in month six to eighteen of phase one, depending on how quickly position is secured.

The men who get through all three phases reliably are not the most talented. They are not the most connected. They are not the best natural entrepreneurs. They are the men who ran the sequence in order and didn't skip ahead.

THIS MINUTE

The pause is available right now.

Not for hours. You don't have hours yet. But five minutes. Before the house wakes up, or after it quiets, or during the commute if the commute is yours alone.

Five minutes to close the calculation loop intentionally, and substitute it for a single question from the reconnaissance list. Not all three questions. One.

What problem do I already know how to solve that other people are still stuck on?

Write one honest answer.

That's it. That's today.

THIS WEEK

Run the full reconnaissance. All three questions, in a physical notebook, over the course of the week.

Monday: What problems do I already know how to solve? Start with the ages-eight-to-twelve question. Write fast. Don't filter.

Wednesday: What could I produce that others would consume?

Friday: Where does my week have real, honest, unallocated hours?

Read what you wrote at the end of the week. Look for the answer that appears in more than one question. The skill that is both something you know how to do and something others consistently bring their problems to you for. That intersection is where to start.

Saturday: Open your notebook to a fresh page and run the Income Inventory. All four columns. Column D — what people ask you for — gets the most time. Write every example you can remember.

If nothing appears in the intersection this week, the reconnaissance wasn't complete. Run it again next week. The answer is there. It usually takes two passes to be honest enough to see it.

THIS MONTH

By the end of this month: one stream identified.

The skill or knowledge you will build the first income stream from. The specific problem it solves. The specific type of person who has that problem. The simplest possible format in which you could begin delivering value.

No investment required yet. No platform required yet. One person in your life who has the problem your capability solves — tell them what you're thinking. Ask them if it would be worth something to them. Their answer is more valuable than any business plan you can write alone.

The pause is working when you're running this reconnaissance instead of the calculation loop. That's how you know you've built enough position to begin the second fight.

The second fight is how this ends differently.

CHAPTER 9
SILENT ISOLATION

"The fight is won or lost far away from witnesses—behind the lines, in the gym, and out there on the road, long before I dance under those lights."

- Muhammad Ali

It's 3 AM again.

You're running the same calculations. The same numbers. The same impossible math.

But this time, what keeps you awake isn't just the numbers.

It's the fact that the person sleeping next to you—or in the next room, or across town during their week with the kids—has no idea how bad it is.

Your spouse asked you last week. "Are we okay? Financially?"

You said yes. "We're fine. Just tight this month."

You lied.

You're not fine. You're $28,000 in debt. The gap between income and expenses is $350 monthly. The emergency fund is $0. One crisis destroys everything.

But you couldn't say that. Couldn't admit it. Because admitting it means admitting you're failing. Admitting you can't handle it. Admitting you're not the provider you're supposed to be.

So you said you're fine. And you carried it alone.

That 3 AM version of you—the one running the numbers alone—deserves better. And better is possible. That's why you're still reading.

Your brother called yesterday. Wanted to grab lunch. You made an excuse. Lunch feels impossible right now. So does being honest about why. This is the weight people carry alone—and it gets heavier every time it goes unsaid.

So you avoid him. Add distance. Protect the secret.

Your coworker mentioned his financial advisor yesterday. Casual conversation. "Yeah, we're putting away about $1,500 a month now. Really trying to catch up on retirement."

You stayed silent. Didn't mention that your retirement contributions are $0. That you're not catching up, you're falling further behind.

You just nodded. Changed the subject. Maintained the appearance.

The family group text is planning the annual gathering. Everyone contributing $200 for the venue and food. The text sits unanswered. $200 isn't there right now—and saying so out loud feels harder than staying quiet. But this silence has a cost too.

So you'll make an excuse last minute. Won't show up. Add more distance.

Every relationship requires either honesty or distance. You chose distance. Because honesty feels impossible.

You're carrying $28,000 in debt, $350 monthly gap, zero buffer, constant stress, and complete isolation.

Eighty—one percent of men say money stress impacts their mental health. More than half haven't told anyone.

You're in the majority. Carrying it alone. In silence. The weight compounding daily.

But you don't have to stay in that majority. One conversation—one honest sentence to one right person—starts changing that today.

The isolation is crushing you.

THE ACTUAL PROBLEM

The problem isn't just that you're struggling financially.

The problem is that you're struggling financially in complete isolation, which makes every other problem worse.

Isolation—carrying it completely alone with no one knowing—compounds paralysis. Every paralysis pattern from Chapter 2 gets worse when you're carrying it alone.

The Overwhelm Cascade: Twelve problems, no external input, no alternative perspectives. Your brain tries to solve all twelve alone. Impossible.

The Perfection Trap: Waiting for perfect plan, no one to reality—check if the plan is actually necessary or if imperfect action would work.

Wrong—Move Paralysis: Terrified of making it worse, no one to tell you if your fear is legitimate or catastrophic thinking.

Path Invisibility: Can't see the route, no one who's walked it before to show you the next step.

Decision Fatigue: Depleted from constant decisions, no one to share the load or make decisions with you.

Shame Silence: Can't talk about the struggle, isolation deepens, shame intensifies, cycle repeats.

Identity Threat: Admitting struggle threatens provider identity, but keeping it secret prevents getting help that would actually preserve provider capacity.

All of it worse alone. All of it compounded by isolation.

You're fighting with one hand tied behind your back. The hand is named "support."

YOU CAN'T GET BETTER ALONE

In martial arts, you can shadow box alone. You can drill techniques alone. You can run alone. You can lift weights alone.

But you can't get better alone.

You need training partners.

Someone to test your technique against resistance—against someone actually fighting back. Someone to show you the holes in your defense—the weaknesses you don't see. Someone to push you harder than you'd push yourself. Someone to correct your form when it's sloppy. Someone to drill with when motivation fades.

Every elite fighter has training partners. Multiple training partners. Different sizes. Different styles. Different strengths.

They spar—practice fight—with people better than them who expose weaknesses. They spar with people worse than them who let them practice offense. They spar with people their same level who push them to their limits.

The training doesn't happen in isolation. It happens in community. In partnership. Through shared struggle and mutual support.

Fighting alone means you only ever fight yourself. You never get tested. You never get corrected. You never get pushed beyond self—imposed limits.

You plateau—stop improving. Stagnate. Eventually regress—get worse.

The same principle applies to your financial fight.

You can budget alone. You can cut expenses alone. You can make plans alone.

But you can't get better alone.

The martial arts sparring partner is sacred. Not because they go easy on you — but because they don't. They test your technique, expose your blind spots, and pressure-test everything you think you know about how to fight. And yet, because you trust them, there's no real defeat at risk. You can throw your best combination, get countered, and learn something — without it costing you the match that matters.

That's what a training partner is in this fight too.

Not a cheerleader. A sparring partner. Someone you can mentally joust with. Someone you can bring your "**confidently wrong**" ideas to — your budget you swore was airtight, your justification for why this expense is different, your plan you've convinced yourself is solid — and have them held up under full light, scrutinized without mercy, returned to you either sharpened or dismantled.

The sparring partner doesn't let you practice against a compliant opponent. They come at you with real questions. *Did you actually do what you said? Is that reasoning sound or are you rationalizing again? You've said this before — what's different this time?*

They don't need to be an expert. They need to be present, honest, and committed to the same fight. A spouse who knows the real numbers. A friend who's also building position. A brother fighting alongside you. Someone from an online community. An accountability partner you found specifically for this purpose.

One person who knows the truth, holds you to your word, and is willing to land the uncomfortable hit when your thinking needs it — not to defeat you, but to make you harder to defeat when it counts.

THE SHAME CYCLE

Shame creates isolation. Isolation creates worse outcomes. Worse outcomes create more shame. The cycle tightens.

The moment you speak it out loud to one trusted person, that cycle begins to break. You don't have to fix everything first. You just have to say it.

You're ashamed that you're $28,000 in debt. So you don't tell anyone. So you have no external input. So you make decisions alone. So you make mistakes you wouldn't make with input. So the situation gets worse. So the shame deepens. So the isolation intensifies.

Shame about debt is almost universal among people who care deeply about providing. The shame means you care. Now let's redirect that energy into movement.

The cycle only breaks when you tell someone.

Not because telling someone magically solves the debt. Because telling someone breaks the isolation that's preventing you from fighting effectively.

When you tell one person the truth things can roller—ball fast:

They reality—check your catastrophic thinking. "You think you're uniquely failing. You're not. This is normal struggle. Ultimately this is what worked for me..." And boom, ideas and inspirations follow.

They provide alternative perspectives. "Have you tried calling the creditor? They might negotiate."

They hold you accountable. "You said you'd cut three subscriptions this week. Did you?"

They notice patterns you miss. "You keep saying you'll build the buffer but then you drain it for things that aren't emergencies. That's the pattern."

They push you when motivation fades. "You committed to this. You said 42 months. You're 8 months in. Keep going."

All of that becomes available when you break the isolation.

None of it exists when you carry it alone.

Research shows accountability partnerships increase execution by 65%. Not because they solve the problem for you. Because they prevent you from quitting when things get hard.

WHO TO TELL

The training partner can't be just anyone. Some people will make it worse. They'll judge. They'll lecture. They'll tell you what you should have done years ago. They'll compare you to themselves. They'll make you feel worse than you already do.

Those aren't training partners. Those are time burglars dressed as helpers.

The right training partner has five specific qualities. Not nice—to—have qualities. Requirements. All five must be present or the partnership fails.

The first quality: They're fighting their own fight. Fighting right now. Currently engaged. Active in their own battle.

This matters because understanding comes from current struggle, not past memory. The person who fought their way out of debt twenty years ago remembers the victory. They've forgotten the daily grind of saying no, the shame of comparison, the weight of carrying it month after month. Memory smooths the rough edges. Makes the hard parts seem easier in retrospect than they were in reality.

But the person fighting right now? They know. They know what it costs to be disciplined when you're exhausted. They know what it feels like to watch everyone else consume while you abstain. They know the weight because they're carrying it.

When you tell them you're struggling, they don't respond with "Just buckle down" or "I did it, you can too." They respond with "I know. I'm doing it right now. It's hard. Keep going."

That's the difference between someone who remembers the fight and someone who's in the fight. One offers platitudes. One offers solidarity.

The person fighting their own fight also has no interest in judging yours. They're too busy deploying their own game-plans to waste energy evaluating whether you're doing it right. They're not looking down at you from solid ground. They're standing next to you in the same mud.

This is why training partners work and mentors serve a different function. The training partner is your peer—same level, same struggle, same daily grind. The mentor is ahead of you—already solid ground, already won the fight you're starting. Both are necessary. But the training partner must be actively fighting, not reminiscing about fights they won years ago.

The second quality: They won't judge you. When you tell them the truth—the factual numbers, the real situation, the shame you're carrying—they receive it without making you feel like a failure.

This doesn't mean they coddle you. Doesn't mean they tell you everything's fine when it's not. Doesn't mean they minimize the severity of your footing.

It means they separate the situation from your identity. They see the debt, the gap, the lack of buffer as problems to solve, not character defects to condemn. They acknowledge the reality without adding shame to the weight you're already carrying.

The wrong person hears your situation and responds with: "How did you let it get this bad?" or "I would never..." or "If you had just..." All of that is judgment. All of it makes you regret sharing. All of it ensures you won't be honest with them again.

The right person hears your situation and responds with: "Okay. That's where you are. What are you doing about it?" No condemnation of how you got there. No comparison to what they would have done. Just acknowledgment of current position and focus on forward movement.

This quality is rare because most people can't separate problem from person. They see financial struggle as moral failure. See debt as character weakness. See lack of discipline as inherent inadequacy.

The right training partner understands that systems fail, not people. That you're not your situation. That where you are now doesn't define who you are or what you're capable of becoming.

When judgment is absent, honesty becomes possible. You can tell them the full truth without filtering, without minimizing, without protecting your image. And that honesty is what makes the partnership functional.

The third quality: They'll tell you the truth. This is the counterbalance to the second quality. They won't judge you, but they also won't lie to protect your feelings.

When you're catastrophizing—inventing disaster scenarios to justify inaction—they call it out. "That's not realistic risk assessment. That's fear keeping you paralyzed. Move anyway."

When you're making excuses—explaining why the book won't work for your unique situation—they cut through it. "Everyone's situation feels unique. The protocol works anyway. do it."

When you're about to revert—relaxing discipline because pressure released temporarily—they see the pattern before you do. "You're doing the thing you said you wouldn't do. The loop is starting again. Stop."

This is truth—telling, not criticism. The difference is intent and delivery.

Criticism tears down: "You always quit when things get hard." Truth—telling builds up: "You're starting to revert to the pattern we talked about. You said you weren't going to do that this time. Stay committed."

The training partner who won't tell you hard truths isn't actually helping you. They're letting you stay comfortable in dysfunction because confronting you feels uncomfortable for them. That's not partnership. That's enabling dressed as support.

The right partner understands that truth serves you even when it stings. That reality—checking your excuses is a gift, not an attack. That pushing back on your rationalizations is exactly what you need when your own brain is working against you.

Musashi wrote about the importance of training partners who attack with real intent. Not partners who let you practice techniques against compliant opponents. Partners who actually try to defeat you so you learn to defend against real attacks, not theoretical ones.

Financial training partners work the same way. The one who tells you comfortable lies isn't preparing you for real struggle. The one who tells you uncomfortable truths is.

The fourth quality: They'll hold you accountable. This is where training partnership becomes tactical support.

You tell them what you're committing to for the week. They check if you did it. That's the mechanism. Simple. Uncomfortable. Necessary.

"This week I'm cutting three subscriptions and listing five items to sell."

Saturday comes. They ask: "Did you cut the three subscriptions? Did you list the five items?"

If yes, they acknowledge the win. "Good. Keep going."

If no, they ask why without accepting excuses. "What stopped you? Is it going to stop you next week? What are you doing differently?"

This is accountability, not interrogation. The difference is they're asking to keep you moving, not to shame you for failing.

Most people don't have this in their lives. Nobody asks them if they did what they said they'd do. Nobody checks. Nobody follows up. So commitments become suggestions. Intentions replace actions. Plans remain incomplete.

The training partner closes that gap. Makes commitment real by adding external consequence. Not punishment. Just the reality that someone will know if you didn't follow through. Someone will ask why. Someone will push you to do better next week.

This external accountability creates a different kind of pressure than internal motivation. Internal motivation fades. External accountability persists whether you feel motivated or not.

You don't want to follow the plan this week? Doesn't matter. Your training partner is checking Saturday. That's enough to get you moving even when motivation is gone. And movement creates momentum. Momentum carries you further than motivation ever could.

The fourth quality makes the partnership functional rather than just supportive. Support without accountability is friendship. Accountability without judgment is partnership.

The fifth quality: They're capable of discretion. What you tell them stays between you and them. Period.

This isn't about formal confidentiality agreements or legal obligation. This is about character. About being the kind of person who can receive sensitive information and not broadcast it.

Your financial situation is not entertainment. Not something to share with others, even in concern, even in prayer requests, even in asking for advice on your behalf. Respect your own privacy and keep some secrets. Training partners and mentors aside, I don't want you look to any and everyone for support. They are unknown quantifiers and are best kept at arms length.

The training partner who can't keep confidence destroys the partnership before it starts. Because the moment you tell them something and it ends up shared with others—no matter how well—intentioned—you stop being honest with them.

Discretion means they don't share what you told them. Don't hint about your struggles to mutual friends. Don't use your situation as an example when talking to others. Don't even acknowledge to others that they know about your financial position.

If someone asks them "How's [your name] doing financially?" the answer is "Ask him" or "I don't know." Not "He's struggling" or "He's working on some things" or any other response that confirms they have information.

This level of discretion is rare. Most people can't hold information without releasing pressure by sharing it. They tell their spouse. They tell their close friend. They mention it in confidence to someone else. Each share dilutes the trust. Each leak makes you less likely to be fully honest.

The training partner capable of complete discretion earns complete honesty in return. You can tell them the numbers without wondering who else will know. You can admit the shame without it becoming public knowledge. You can be vulnerable without it being used against you later.

This fifth quality protects all the others. Without discretion, the partnership can't function because you'll never tell them the full truth. With discretion, the partnership becomes a safe space to be completely honest about the fight you're actually in.

These five qualities together—not separately—create functional training partnership. Missing one quality compromises the whole system.

They must be fighting their own fight AND not judge you AND tell you truth AND hold you accountable AND keep confidence. All five. Not four out of five. All five.

This is why the right training partner is hard to find. Why you might have to search intentionally rather than assuming someone in your life already qualifies. Why online communities sometimes provide better partnerships than local relationships.

But when you find someone with all five qualities, the partnership becomes force multiplication. You reach further with them than you could alone. They see patterns you miss. They push you harder than you'd push yourself. They prevent reverting before it starts. They hold you to commitments you'd let slide if only you were watching.

Find your training partner. Verify all five qualities are present. Build the partnership intentionally. Then use it to win the fight you're in.

If you're single, divorced, or estranged from family, the training partner might be someone you find online. Forums exist. Support groups exist. Communities of people fighting the same fight exist.

You don't need a lifelong friend. You need someone who can receive truth and give accountability.

One person. That's the requirement.

SOLO PLAN

You're not announcing your financial situation to everyone. You're telling one person the specific truth.

Not "money's tight." Specific: "I have $28,000 in debt, $350 monthly gap, zero buffer. I'm executing the protocols from a book. I need someone who knows the real situation and asks me weekly if I'm doing what I said I'd do."

The specificity—being exact, detailed—matters. Vague admission produces vague support.

"Money's tight" gets "Yeah, it's tough for everyone right now."

Specific numbers get real engagement. "Okay. What's the plan? What are you doing this week? When do I check in?"

The training partner needs the authentic state to provide needed support.

Here's the conversation framework:

"I need to tell you something. It's financial. It's not good. I'm not looking for advice or judgment. I'm looking for accountability."

They'll either engage or they won't. If they won't, wrong person. Find different person.

If they engage:

"I have [specific amount] in debt. My monthly gap is [specific amount]. I have [specific amount] in buffer. I'm executing a system to fix this over [specific dates]. I need you to know the truth and check in with me weekly. Can you do that?"

If yes, you have your training partner.

Then you establish the outline:

"Every Sunday evening, I'll text you what I'm committing to for the week. Every Saturday, you ask me if I did it. That's it. You don't need to solve it. You just need to know the truth and hold me to my word."

Simple. Clear. Specific.

One person. One truth. One accountability mechanism.

THE DIGITAL CORNER MAN

Before we leave this chapter, there's a tool worth addressing directly. You've heard of it. You may already use it. Artificial intelligence — AI — is now capable of conversation sophisticated enough that some men will consider using it as a substitute for the training partner we've been discussing.

I want to give you an honest assessment. Not a dismissal. Not uncritical enthusiasm. An honest look at what AI can do in this fight and where it categorically cannot go.

Because the answer is not simple, and you deserve the real version.

WHAT AI CAN DO

A corner man in boxing doesn't fight. He doesn't take the punches. He sits outside the ropes and watches — sees things the fighter can't see from inside the action — and between rounds he delivers precise, rapid information designed to keep the fighter alive and winning.

That's closer to what AI is than most people realize.

AI can hold your numbers without judgment. You can type your actual debt balance — the real one, not the rounded-down version you've been telling yourself — at 2 AM on a Tuesday when shame is loudest and no human is available. It won't flinch. It won't go quiet. It won't change the subject. It receives the information and responds to the information.

For the man who has told no one, who has carried the real numbers in complete silence for years, this matters. Speaking the truth — even to a machine — is practice for speaking it to a person. The words become less impossible when you've already said them once.

AI can work the protocol with you. Every SOP in this book can be applied in conversation with an AI. Walk through This Minute. Build the gap calculation. Map the debt snowball. Run the income inventory. The AI will follow the logic, catch mathematical errors, and ask the questions the protocol requires. It doesn't get distracted. It doesn't bring its own financial anxiety to your session. It stays focused on your fight.

AI can reality-check catastrophizing. When your brain runs the worst-case calculations at 3 AM and arrives at disaster as the only possible outcome, AI can interrupt that loop. Feed it the actual numbers and ask for an honest assessment. It will tell you what the data shows, not what your fear is projecting. That's valuable at 2 AM when no human training partner is available and the spiral is starting.

AI can hold your commitments. You can tell it what you're committing to this week. You can come back Saturday and report honestly. It will ask whether you did what you said. It won't let you slide past a non-answer. It will ask again. That mechanism — someone asking if you did what you said — is available to you at any hour, any day, at no cost, with no social risk.

AI can help you prepare to talk to a human. Write out what you're going to say to your training partner before you say it. Work through how to tell your spouse the real numbers. Practice the conversation until the words stop closing your throat. Use the AI as a rehearsal space before you step into the real thing.

These are real capabilities. Don't dismiss them.

WHAT AI CANNOT DO

Now the honest part.

Go back to the five qualities of a real training partner. Run AI against each one.

Quality One: They're fighting their own fight.

AI has never carried debt. It has never watched its daughter's face fall and known it was the gap that put that look there. It has never sat in a parking lot before going inside because it needed sixty seconds to get its face right before the family saw it. It has never had the cortisol of financial stress in its body at 3 AM. It has never felt the weight of providing and falling short simultaneously.

It knows about these things. It can describe them with precision because it has processed more human testimony about financial stress than any single human could read in a lifetime. But knowing about the fight and being in the fight are not the same thing.

When your real training partner says "I know. It's hard. Keep going" — they know because they're in it. The knowledge is carried in the body, not just the mind. That's not a small distinction. That is the entire distinction.

AI cannot say "I know" and mean what a human means when they say it. It can say the words. The words are hollow in a way that matters when you're at the bottom of the loop and need someone to confirm that what you're carrying is real and survivable.

Quality Two: They won't judge you.

AI passes this one technically. No judgment. But the absence of judgment in AI comes from the absence of stakes. A human training partner chooses not to judge you despite having the capacity to do so — that choice is meaningful. AI cannot judge you the way a human can, which means its non-judgment costs nothing and signals nothing. It is the difference between a man choosing to trust you with difficult information and a machine that cannot betray you because it has no self-interest. Both feel like safety but they are not the same safety.

Quality Three: They'll tell you the truth.

AI will tell you what the numbers show. It will call out logical inconsistencies. It will identify when your reasoning doesn't hold. That's useful.

What it cannot do is read what you're not saying. The human training partner who has known you for years notices when your voice goes flat, when you change the subject faster than usual, when the confidence in your answer doesn't match the words. They hear the thing underneath the thing. They ask the question you didn't realize you were avoiding.

AI only knows what you put in front of it. You control the information. Which means you can manage what the AI sees without even meaning to — because the parts of the truth that are hardest to face are often the parts you won't type first. The human training partner who knows you doesn't give you that escape.

Quality Four: They'll hold you accountable.

This is where AI has the most structural limitation.

Real accountability has initiation. Your training partner texts you Saturday morning whether you opened the conversation or not. The check-in arrives whether you're ready for it or whether you've been avoiding it all week. That arrival — unsolicited, on schedule, regardless of your readiness — is the mechanism. That is what makes commitment real.

AI waits. It does not initiate. It does not text you Saturday morning. It sits until you open it, which means the man most in need of accountability — the one avoiding the check-in, the one who hasn't looked at his numbers in two weeks, the one who made three impulse purchases and hasn't told anyone — that man simply doesn't open it. The accountability only functions when you choose to engage it. And the days when you most need accountability are the days you're least likely to make that choice.

The human training partner cannot be avoided this way. That unavoidability is not a flaw in the design. It is the entire point.

Quality Five: Discretion.

AI keeps nothing and tells no one. On that specific measure it is perfect. What you type stays between you and the session. No one finds out.

But discretion in the human training partner context means something deeper than silence. It means someone who chose to carry your burden privately out of respect for you as a man. That choice — made by a person with the capacity to tell others and the social incentive to do so — is an act of loyalty. It strengthens the bond. It creates the kind of trust that deepens over time.

AI silence is not loyalty. It is architecture.

THE HONEST POSITION

Use AI as a bridge, not a destination.

If you have not yet found your training partner — if the shame is still too acute, if you live somewhere isolated, if you haven't identified the right person yet — AI is available tonight. Right now. At no cost. With no social risk. Use it to say the numbers out loud for the first time. Use it to work the protocol. Use it to prepare for the human conversation you need to have.

But understand what you're doing when you do that. You're using a tool to get ready for the real thing. You are not doing the real thing.

A man who does pull-ups alone in his garage has built some strength. He is better prepared than a man who did nothing. But he has not sparred. He has not been hit. He does not know how he responds under real pressure because real pressure requires another person who can genuinely threaten you — whose force is real, whose intent is real, whose resistance comes from their own will and not from your input.

Financial accountability works the same way. AI can prepare you. It cannot replace what happens when a real person who knows your real numbers asks you a real question on a Saturday morning when you don't want to answer it.

The man who uses AI and calls it a training partner is the man doing pull-ups in the garage and calling it sparring. He has worked. He is not ready.

Use the tool. Build the bridge. Then cross it.

Find the human.

THE MENTOR

The training partner holds you accountable. The mentor—someone ahead of you who's already done what you're trying to do—shows you the path.

Different roles. Both necessary.

The training partner is your peer. Someone fighting the same fight at roughly the same level. They check if you're executing. They reality—check your thinking. They prevent reverting.

The mentor is ahead of you. They've already walked the path you're starting. They have the results you're trying to achieve. They know what works because they've done it.

You need both.

In martial arts, you need training partners at your level to spar with. You also need an instructor who's already earned their black belt—the highest rank, showing mastery—who knows techniques you don't, who can correct your form before bad habits set in.

The training partner pushes you. The mentor guides you.

Same principle applies here.

You need someone who's already closed the gap, eliminated the debt, built the buffer, solid ground. Someone with genuine results. Not someone who read about it or has theories. Someone who's done it.

Then you glue yourself to them—stick as close as they'll allow.

FINDING THE MENTOR

The mentor must have results. Proven results. Consistent results.

Not someone who got lucky once. Not someone who inherited wealth. Not someone with a high income who never had to fight. Someone who started from struggle and built position through discipline and performance.

The person who makes $150,000 and has always made $150,000 can't mentor you. They never fought your fight. Different battlefield entirely.

The person who made $45,000, closed a $400 monthly gap, eliminated $35,000 in debt, and built six months of buffer over five years? That person can mentor you. They have the results. They walked the path.

Where do you find them?

In your life if you're lucky. Coworker who mentioned they paid off debt. Friend who's obviously financially secure but didn't start that way. Family member who rebuilt after bankruptcy—after declaring they couldn't pay debts. Someone who has what you're building.

In communities if not in your life. Online forums for debt management. Financial independence communities. Support groups. People posting results—true numbers, real timelines, substantive methods.

Through asking directly. "You mentioned you paid off $40,000 in debt. How did you do it? Can I ask you questions as I go through this?"

Most people who've done hard things are willing to help someone else do the same hard things. If they say no, wrong person. Ask someone else.

When you find the right person, approach with humility and respect for their time. Don't just ask what they can do for you. Understand that mentorship is a gift, not an entitlement. Consider how you could add something to their life and offer it. Ask if they see how you can contribute to their lives.

If you can provide value first—even something small—do it. Maybe they mention a project. Maybe you can help. Maybe you know someone they should meet. Lead with service when possible, even in small ways.

The mentor who sees you're willing to give, not just take, is more likely to invest their time in you. If they agree, glue yourself hip to hip with their wisdom and methodologies.

GLUE YOURSELF

As much as they'll let you without driving them off.

You're not asking for casual advice. You're asking for mentorship. Regular access. Real guidance.

"I'm executing a debt elimination plan. You've done this already. Can I check in with you monthly to make sure I'm on the right path? Can I ask you questions when I get stuck?"

If they say yes, you take that seriously.

You show up when you say you will. You produce what they suggest. You don't waste their time. You respect that they're giving you access to knowledge they earned through years of discipline.

Monthly check—in. Fifteen minutes. You come prepared.

"Here's where I was last month. Here's what I did. Here's where I am now. Here's what I'm planning next. Am I on track? What am I missing?"

They tell you. You listen. You earn their respect by producing tangible results. You report back next month.

The white belt's job is to absorb. At this stage, their results speak louder than your reasoning. Stay humble, stay coachable—opinions earn weight after results and performance prove your theories.

MODEL COMPLETELY

The mentor has results you want. They got those results through specific behaviors, specific thinking, specific habits. Model all of it.

Don't cherry-pick the parts that seem reasonable and skip the parts that feel extreme. If they tracked every expense daily, you track every expense daily. If they cut lifestyle to near-austerity for three years while attacking debt, you do the same. If they checked the budget every Sunday morning, you check the budget every Sunday morning. They got results doing it. You want results. Do it exactly as they did it.

This is Shu Ha Ri from Chapter 1. You're in Shu—the copying stage. No improvisation. No adapting to your preferences. No "I'll do a version of this that works better for me." Later, after you have results, you can adapt. Not now. Now you follow.

The same principle applies to your conversations with them. You discuss what they want to discuss—not what you want to discuss. If they want to talk about cutting subscriptions when you wanted to ask about investment strategies, you talk about cutting subscriptions. Investment comes later. They're talking about subscriptions because that's what matters at your stage. They know this because they've been where you are.

Your white belt brain thinks it knows what's important. It doesn't. That's why you're white belt. Their black belt brain knows what's important. That's why they have results.

When they talk, you listen. You take notes. You ask clarifying questions about execution only—how exactly did you do it, what did you use, what time of day. Ask how, not why. Save questions about your unique circumstances for after the fundamentals are proven.

Match their intensity completely. The mentor who eliminated $35,000 in debt in 42 months wasn't casual about it. They were intense, focused, and disciplined every day for 42 months. That's the intensity you match—not your comfortable intensity, theirs.

Find what fueled them through it. Kids. Pride. Fear of the alternative. Find their fuel and use it as your own.

You model. You achieve. You report results.

THE MENTOR IS NOT YOUR FRIEND

The mentor might become your friend. But that's not the relationship you're building.

You're building a teacher—student relationship. They teach. You learn.

The training partner is your peer. You're equals fighting the samq fight. That relationship can be friendship.

The mentor is ahead of you. You're not equals. Not yet. Maybe after you have results. Not now.

This might feel uncomfortable. You're used to egalitarian relationships —everyone equal. Everyone's opinion matters equally. Everyone's perspective is valid.

Not here. Not in this relationship.

Their opinion matters because they have results. Your opinion doesn't matter because you don't have results yet.

That's not cruel. That's accurate.

The white belt doesn't argue with the black belt about technique. The white belt shuts up and learns.

You're white belt. Financially speaking.

The person who eliminated debt and built position is black belt.

Act accordingly.

Respect the hierarchy. Respect the results. Respect the knowledge they earned.

Listen more than you talk. Act more than you question. Model more than you modify.

After you have results, your opinions gain weight. After you've eliminated your debt and built your buffer and secured your footing, then you can have conversations as equals.

Not before.

WHEN YOU CAN'T FIND A MENTOR

You might not have access to someone who's done this.

Then you use this book as your mentor. You use the protocols as the SOP to model.

The book gives you the exact methods. The specific steps. The proven strategies.

Follow them exactly. Don't modify. Don't adapt to your preferences. Perform as written.

This minute. This week. This month. Repeat for 42 months.

The book is the black belt instructor when you can't find a human one.

But if you can find a human mentor with proven results, take that opportunity. Human mentorship beats book knowledge because humans can answer your specific questions, correct your specific mistakes, and push you harder than you'll push yourself.

Find them if you can. Model them completely. Match their intensity. Get their results.

SOP: THIS MINUTE

Identify one person you could tell.

Not the perfect person. Not your ideal training partner. One solid person who exists in your life right now who might be capable of receiving truth and providing accountability.

Write their name down.

Potential training partner: __________

If you can identify someone who's already done this—someone who's eliminated debt, built buffer, solid ground—write their name as potential mentor.

Potential mentor: _________

If you can't identify anyone for either role, write: "Online community / Support group / Find someone"

You've identified the people or the path to finding the people.

SOP: THIS WEEK

You're going to break the silence with one person.

Monday: Decide who you're telling. The training partner you identified or someone else. Lock it in. This is who you're telling this week.

Tuesday: Script the conversation. Write down what you're going to say. "I need to tell you something about my financial situation. It's not good. I'm not looking for advice or judgment. I'm looking for accountability." Practice saying it out loud. Alone. Until it doesn't feel impossible.

Wednesday: Set up the conversation. Text them or call them. "Can we talk this week? In person if possible, phone if not. I need to tell you something." Don't explain yet. Just set the time.

Thursday or Friday: Have the conversation. Tell them the truth. Specific numbers. Specific plan. Specific ask: "I need you to check in with me weekly about whether I'm executing."

Saturday: Send them your first weekly commitment. "This week I'm committing to: [specific actions from current chapter protocol]. Check with me next Saturday if I did it."

Sunday: Review the week. You broke the silence. One person knows. The isolation is broken. If you identified a potential mentor, reach out.

"I saw that you eliminated debt. I'm starting that fight now. Can I ask you questions as I go through this?"

The secret is shared. The accountability exists. The mentor contact is made if available.

SOP: THIS MONTH

You're going to build the accountability relationship and potentially the mentor relationship.

Week 1: run this WEEK. Tell one person. Establish check—in. Contact potential mentor if available.

Week 2: Execute your weekly commitment. Whatever you told your training partner you'd do. Do it. When they check in Saturday, you have honest answer: "Yes, I did it" or "No, I didn't, here's why."

If mentor responded positively, schedule first check—in. Monthly. Fifteen minutes. Come prepared with numbers and questions.

Week 3: Continue weekly commitments. If mentor check—in happened, apply all that they suggested. Don't modify. Don't debate. Do exactly as they describe.

Week 4: Continue weekly commitments. By week four, the pattern is establishing with your training partner. They ask. You answer. You commit to next week. Repeat.

If you had mentor check—in, prepare for next month's check—in. Track results. Note questions that came up.

By month's end, weekly accountability running with training partner. Monthly guidance from mentor if available. The isolation is broken. The support structure exists.

THE RESISTANCE

Every excuse you're generating right now is the isolation protecting itself. You've already named the pattern. Don't obey it.

TACTICAL OVERRIDE

You're in Week 2. You're supposed to have the conversation with one person.

You can't. The fear is too intense. The shame is crushing. Every time you try to speak the words, your throat closes. You're frozen.

That feeling—the throat-closing, frozen, can't-say-it feeling—is not weakness. It's the body protecting something it thinks can't survive the truth. It can. You can.

Stop trying to have the verbal conversation. Start with written words.

Write the truth down. Not for them yet. For you.

Open a document. A note on your phone. Piece of paper. Whatever.

Write: "My financial situation right now:"

Then write the numbers. All of them.

Total debt: $______

Monthly gap: $______

Buffer amount: $______

Months of runway: ______

Write what you're doing about it:

"I'm executing: [Chapter protocols you're on]"

Write what you need:

"I need someone to know this and check in weekly if I'm doing what I said I'd do."

Now you have it written. Specific. Clear. True.

Send it. Text. Email. Message. However you communicate with the person.

Don't call. Don't meet in person yet. Just send the written truth.

"I wrote this out because I couldn't say it out loud yet. Read it. Let me know if you can help with weekly check—ins."

The written word breaks the verbal paralysis.

Most people can write what they can't say. Write it first. Send it. Then have the follow—up conversation after they've read it and responded.

Physical writing breaks the paralysis of speaking.

And once the truth is written and sent, the secret is broken. The isolation is broken. The training partner knows.

From there, you build the verbal accountability. But the written truth gets you started.

THE MARRIED/PARTNERED SITUATION

If you have a spouse or partner, they're the first choice for training partner—and the hardest conversation you'll have in this entire campaign.

Most men hide financial reality from their partners. The objections come fast: *I don't want to worry them. They'll blame me. It will cause fights. They don't need to know the details.*

None of it holds. They're already worried—they can sense something's wrong, and uncertainty is worse than truth. You can't fix a situation while hiding it from the person sharing the consequences. Fighting about the truth is better than living in the deception. If the situation affects both of you, they need to know so they can fight with you instead of in the dark.

The conversation might be brutal. Have it anyway. Continued deception while the situation deteriorates destroys relationships more surely than honest admission.

The opener is different from the SOLO PLAN framework—not "I'm struggling" but "I've been hiding this from you":

"I need to tell you the truth about our financial situation. It's worse than I've let on. I've been carrying this alone and I can't anymore. Here are the numbers. Here's what I'm doing about it. I need you to know, and I need us to fight this together."

Then the same framework: specifics, questions answered, weekly transparency committed to.

Might save the relationship. Might reveal the relationship can't survive honesty. Either outcome is better than continued deception.

THE SINGLE/DIVORCED SITUATION

If you're single or divorced, no one in your immediate circle may qualify—or exist. That's fine. Find someone specifically for this purpose.

Online communities exist for exactly this fight. Search: *"Debt payoff accountability partner," "financial accountability group," "budget accountability community."* Find one person also looking for weekly accountability. Partner with them.

They don't need to be local. They don't need to be a friend. The relationship doesn't need to be deep. It needs to be functional:

Sunday: *"This week I'm committing to X, Y, Z."* Saturday: *"Did you do it?"* Repeat.

Someone who knows your numbers and asks if you did what you said. That's the entire requirement. Don't let "I don't have someone in my life" become the excuse that keeps you isolated. The person exists online. Go find them.

THE FINAL ISOLATION

Some men will read this entire book, execute every protocol, fight every fight, and still refuse to tell anyone.

They'll do it alone. They'll succeed or fail alone. They'll carry the entire burden in silence because admitting struggle feels impossible.

That's the final isolation. The choice to keep the secret even when breaking it would help.

Musashi: "It is better to have one friend of great value than many friends who are good for nothing."

One friend. One training partner. One person who knows.

That's all you need. Not many. One.

Add a mentor if you can find one. Someone ahead of you on the path. Someone with proven results.

If you finish this book and still haven't told anyone, you're choosing unnecessary hardship.

You're fighting with one hand tied behind your back because you refuse to untie it.

You're better than that choice.

WHO'S NEXT

The weight of carrying this quietly—It's one of the seven patterns that keep men frozen. The shame silence that makes the problem feel more permanent than it is because you've never said it to another person who has been through it.

One conversation changes this. Not therapy, not a financial advisor, not a support group. One honest conversation with one person who will ask you every week whether you did what you said you'd do. That's the entire structure. It's available to you right now.

The next chapter is where everything you've read becomes a decision. Not a plan to act someday—a decision about whether you'll act today.

CHAPTER 10
THE DECISION

"In any moment of decision, the best thing you can do is the right thing, the next best thing is the wrong thing, and the worst thing you can do is nothing." - Theodore Roosevelt

You've been reading about yourself.

Nine chapters of watching yourself in a mirror you didn't choose to stand in front of.

That's not comfortable. I know it isn't. The men who get the most out of this book are the ones it made the most uncomfortable — because discomfort is what recognition feels like. You can't be uncomfortable about something that doesn't apply to you.

So let me be direct with you about where we are.

You now understand what's happening and why. You understand the gap — where it came from, how it grows, why it doesn't fix itself. You understand the buffer — what it changes, what it costs to not have it. You understand the debt — the math behind the minimum payments, the years those payments consume, the system designed to keep you paying indefinitely. You understand the retirement problem — the compound effect working against you for every month you delay. You understand fragility — what it looks like when one crisis hits a position with no reserves. You understand the comparison trap and the isolation that makes all of it worse.

You understand the system that's been running underneath your decisions without your knowledge or consent, producing outcomes you didn't choose but have been living with.

None of that understanding cost you anything yet.

Understanding is free. It changes nothing on its own. The man who reads this entire book and closes it unchanged has spent some hours. That's all. The debt is still the debt.

This is the chapter where understanding stops being enough.

"The most difficult thing is the decision to act. The rest is merely tenacity."

- Amelia Earhart

STALLED IN THE PARKING LOT

I want to tell you about a pattern of perpetual failure.

He reads. He recognizes himself. He feels the urgency. The understanding lands — really lands — and for a moment the path is clear. He can see it. And then he closes the book.

Not because he decided not to do it. He never decides not to do it. That's the part that matters. He doesn't sit down and consciously choose inaction. He just doesn't begin. He carries the intention forward with him into the next day, and the day after that, and the day after that. The intention stays intact. The urgency fades. The clarity that felt absolute at the moment of recognition gets softer at the edges as life continues — the job, the kids, the noise, the fatigue. By week two the path that was clear is theoretical again. By month two he barely remembers what it felt like to see it that clearly.

He didn't fail. He postponed. And postponement, held long enough, is the same outcome.

I've watched this happen to men who were more motivated than you are right now. Men who cried reading parts of this. Men who texted me after finishing the first chapter. Men who told their wives something was going to change. Not weak men. Not men who didn't care. Men who cared enormously and still didn't begin.

Because caring isn't the same as moving. Intending isn't the same as starting. Feeling the urgency isn't the same as acting before it fades.

WHAT THIS MOMENT ACTUALLY IS

You are sitting at the exact point where every man who has ever changed his financial position once sat.

Not before reading the information. After. With the information in his head and the familiar weight of his situation still on his chest and the question of whether this time is actually different hanging in the air.

He could not feel the significance of that moment from inside it. Nobody can. The moments that change the trajectory of a life don't announce themselves. They don't feel cinematic. They feel like a Tuesday evening with the book in your lap and the television on in the other room and the refrigerator making that sound it's been making for two weeks.

What made those moments pivots wasn't how they felt. It was what the man did in the next ten minutes.

This is yours.

Not next week when you've had time to think about it. Not after the holidays when things settle down. Not when you feel more ready — that feeling doesn't come. Men who wait to feel ready wait forever. Readiness comes from moving, not before it.

What are you going to do in the next ten minutes?

THE MAN YOU WERE BEFORE YOU READ THIS

He didn't have the information. That was his excuse, and it was a legitimate one. He couldn't see the system running under his decisions. He didn't understand the gap, the buffer, the debt sequence, the compound problem. He was fighting with his hands behind his back and didn't know it.

From this page forward, ignorance is no longer available to you as an explanation. The information is in your head. The system is visible. The path is mapped. If the situation doesn't change from here, it won't be because you didn't know what to do.

That is a harder place to stand than before you opened the first chapter. The man who doesn't know can tell himself the story that he would have if only he'd known. You no longer have that story.

This is the weight of understanding. It removes the comfortable excuse. It puts the responsibility exactly where it belongs: on the decision you make tonight, and the one you make tomorrow morning, and the ones you make every day for the next forty-two months.

I'm not going to dress that up. It's a long time. It's a hard road. There are going to be months where the progress is invisible, where the sacrifice feels disproportionate to the result, where someone around you does something that triggers the comparison and the inadequacy and the pressure to match them. There are going to be moments — maybe many of them — where stopping feels more reasonable than continuing.

I need you to understand something about those moments before you reach them.

DISCIPLINE THAT OUTLASTS MOTIVATION

Motivation is a feeling. Feelings are temporary. Every man who has ever successfully executed a forty-two month financial campaign ran out of motivation somewhere between month three and month eight. Without exception.

The ones who finished didn't finish because they found a way to sustain the feeling. They finished because they built something sturdier than a feeling to carry them through the months when the feeling was gone.

Discipline is a structure. A system of commitments, habits, and accountability that runs regardless of how you feel about it on any given Tuesday. The SOP doesn't care whether you're motivated. It doesn't require enthusiasm. It requires execution. Same moves, same sequence, same tracking, same check-in with the person who knows you're running this — regardless of whether that day feels like forward momentum or like grinding concrete with your bare hands.

This is the thing the men who drift never build. They rely on the feeling to carry them. The feeling sustains them for a while — sometimes months. Then life happens. The motivation takes a hit. Without the structure underneath it, they slow. Then stop. Then tell themselves they're still running it because they never formally quit.

They're not running it. They've stopped. They just haven't admitted it yet.

The drift happens in increments so small they're nearly invisible. The weekly budget review goes monthly. The check-in with the accountability partner gets skipped once, then twice. One purchase gets rationalized — a small one, a justified one, a deserved one — and then the standard for what's justified loosens by a fraction. Then a little more.

Nobody decides to abandon the campaign. They stop defending it against the thousand small compromises that erode it from the outside. Six months later they're back where they started, still carrying the intention, still believing they're the kind of man who would do this — but not doing it.

The protection against drift is not willpower. Willpower is a resource and it depletes. The protection against drift is the number you track and the person who asks whether you hit it.

One number. Written down tonight. Tracked every month for forty-two months. Your monthly gap. Your buffer balance. Your total debt. Pick the one that most clearly shows whether you're moving or standing still. Write it down. That number is your compass in the months when everything else is uncertain.

One person who knows. Not a financial advisor. Not a therapist. Someone in your life who will ask the hard question straight — did you do what you said you'd do this week — and won't let you off the hook when the answer is no. Tell them tonight. Give them the number. Tell them you'll check in with them in thirty days.

These two things — the number and the person — are the difference between a man who executes and a man who intends to.

BEFORE YOU TURN THE PAGE

Every man who has walked this path remembers one thing about the moment he started.

And it opened with one small action. It was the first subscription he canceled. The ten dollars he moved to a separate account. The text he sent to the person who became his accountability partner. The date he wrote on paper — forty-two months from that day — and put somewhere he'd see it every morning.

Something physical. Something that existed in the world instead of only in his head. Something that made the decision real before he could talk himself out of it.

Set up the automatic transfer tonight. Log into your bank and schedule any amount — ten dollars, fifty, whatever the gap currently allows — to move from checking to a separate savings account the day after your next paycheck lands. Automatic. Scheduled. Running without your participation. That account is your buffer. It builds whether you feel like it or not. That's the point.

Or send the text. Right now, before you read another word. Pick up your phone and text your person. Tell them you started. Tell them you'll check in in thirty days with a number. One sentence. That sentence makes the commitment external. You are no longer only accountable to yourself — which means you are no longer only accountable to a man who is very good at forgiving himself for small delays.

Or write the date. Forty-two months from today. Calculate it. Write it on paper — actual paper — and put it where you'll see it when you wake up. Not as decoration. As a deadline. The campaign has an end date. Write it down so it stops being abstract and starts being a day on the calendar you are moving toward.

Either you're moving or you're not. There's no partial version of this that works.

WHAT THE NEXT CHAPTER SHOWS YOU

Chapter 11 is the campaign in full. Month by month. What changes, what holds, what tests you, what proves the system works when you can't feel it working.

It assumes you just did something in the last ten minutes.

If you did — if you set the transfer, sent the text, or wrote the date — then everything that follows is the execution of a decision you've already made. The campaign is already underway. You're not planning to change your financial position anymore.

SOP: THIS MINUTE

Write down one number. Your actual number, not the version that makes it look slightly better. Monthly gap, buffer balance, or total debt — whichever most clearly shows where you stand right now. Date it. This is your baseline. Every measurement for the next forty-two months is relative to this one.

Now do one physical thing from the three options above. Automatic transfer. Text to your person. The date on paper. One of them. Before this chapter ends.

If you reach the end of this minute without having done one of those things, go back and do it. The book will still be here. This decision won't wait indefinitely.

SOP: THIS WEEK

Monday: Execute the commitment action. If you did it in the last ten minutes, it's done. If not, Monday is the deadline. No extensions.

Tuesday: Identify your starting chapter. Gap still open — Chapter Four. Gap closed, no buffer — Chapter Three. Gap closed, buffer exists, debt is the problem — Chapter Five. Re-read only that chapter's SOP section. That's your week-one protocol.

Wednesday: Tell your accountability person the number you're tracking and the chapter you're executing. Not a long conversation. One message, one number, one chapter. Accountability starts with contact.

Thursday: Take one action from your starting chapter's SOP. Not the whole SOP. One action. Today. The purpose is to be moving before the week ends, not planning to move next week.

Friday: Check in with your accountability person. One number. One update. Did you do what you said? Yes or no. If yes, say so. If no, say that too. Honesty is the mechanism. It only works if you use it.

Saturday: Run your number again. Write it down next to Monday's baseline. The difference — up or down, by how much — is your first data point. One data point means nothing by itself. It's the beginning of a record. The record is what carries you through the months when you can't feel the progress.

Sunday: Rest. The campaign is forty-two months. It is not won or lost this week. What matters this week is that you are moving — imperfectly, with incomplete information, against resistance. That's the only kind of movement that actually exists.

SOP: THIS MONTH

Week 1: Run this week completely. Commitment action set. Starting chapter identified. Accountability person told. One action taken. Number tracked. That sequence, executed honestly, is the foundation everything else builds on.

Week 2: Execute your starting chapter's SOP in full for the first time. Not partially. Not the comfortable parts. In full. Copy the moves exactly before you understand why they work. Understanding comes from doing, not from planning to do.

Week 3: Run your number for the second time this month. Write it next to week one. Show it to your accountability person in your check-in. What moved. What didn't. What the next week looks like. The conversation doesn't need to be long. It needs to be honest.

Week 4: Calculate total movement from day one to day thirty. That's your month-one result. Not a feeling about how it went — a number showing what changed. That number is your first piece of evidence. Evidence is what replaces motivation when motivation is gone. Hold onto it.

CHAPTER 11
THE CAMPAIGN

"No battle plan survives first contact with the enemy." - Helmuth von Moltke

You chose Answer One. Full commitment. Ships burned.

Good.

Now let me show you what you're walking into. What happens month by month, year by year, when you run this system completely.

Every phase of this campaign vectors toward the same objective: financial security that doesn't require constant defending. But you don't aim at the objective directly. You aim at the next way point.

The campaign ahead is three and a half years. That's if you deliver perfectly with no major setbacks. Some people take longer. Unexpected job loss extends it. Major medical emergency extends it. Life happens and timelines adjust. We need to plan for a sustained offensive across multiple years.

You need to understand what that actually means before you start. Let me show you a historical parallel that illustrates sequential delivery.

SIEGE OF TYRE

In 332 BC. Alexander the Great has conquered most of the known world. City after city has fallen to his army. He's relentless.

Then he reaches Tyre.

Tyre is a city on an island half a mile from shore. Fortified walls. Supplied by sea. Defended by the Phoenician navy, the best naval force in the world. The city has never been conquered. Ever. Previous sieges lasted years and failed.

Alexander's army is designed for land warfare. He has no navy to match the Phoenicians. He can stand on the shore and look at his objective, but he can't reach it. Can't attack it. Can't conquer it.

Most commanders would have bypassed Tyre. Moved on to easier targets. Declared victory over what they'd already conquered and avoided the hard fight.

Alexander doesn't bypass it. He needs Tyre for strategic reasons—it controls shipping lanes, it's a potential base for Persian naval power if left unconquered.

But he can't attack it directly. Not yet. He doesn't have the capability.

So he builds it.

He orders his army to construct a causeway from the mainland to the island. A land bridge half a mile long. Using stones, timber, rubble from a destroyed city on the shore.

The Tyrians attack the causeway while it's being built. They send fire ships to burn the siege towers. They rain missiles on the workers. Alexander's men die building this causeway. Hundreds of them.

But they keep building. Every day. For seven months.

Seven months of building a causeway under constant enemy fire before they can launch the planned attack.

Most armies would have quit. Would have said "this is taking too long." Would have decided the objective wasn't worth the preparation cost.

Alexander's army keeps building.

Month four: The causeway is halfway done. Progress is visible but the objective is still unreachable. Tyrians still attacking. Men still dying.

Month six: The causeway reaches three-quarters distance. Close enough to see the walls clearly. Close enough to feel like the hard part is done. But the final quarter-mile is the hardest—deeper water, stronger defenses.

Month seven: The causeway reaches the walls. Finally. After seven months of building under fire, they can launch the assault.

The siege engines roll across the causeway. The towers rise against the walls. The army that spent seven months building can now attack.

Tyre falls in weeks once the causeway reaches the walls. The battle itself is almost anticlimactic compared to the seven-month preparation.

Here's why this matters for you:

Your debt is Tyre. Your objective. The thing you want to eliminate.

But you can't attack it directly. Not yet. You don't have the capability. You have a gap that prevents any progress. No buffer to protect against setbacks. No infrastructure to sustain an attack.

You have to build the causeway first.

Closing the gap is building the causeway. Building the infrastructure that makes the objective reachable.

Building the buffer is building the causeway. Creating the protection that lets you sustain the attack when you launch it.

You'll spend months building this infrastructure before you can attack your primary objective. Months of work that doesn't feel like progress toward debt elimination. Months where you can see the objective—debt freedom—but can't reach it yet.

Most people quit during the causeway-building phase. They get frustrated that they're not attacking debt directly. They abandon the SOP because "it's taking too long" or "I'm not seeing results fast enough."

They're standing on the shore demanding to attack the island without building the approach first.

It doesn't work. You need the causeway before you can win the siege.

That's what this chapter shows you. The causeway-building phase. The attack phase. The securing phase. All of it. In sequence. With timeline and expectations accurate to what actually happens.

YEAR ONE: THE FOUNDATION FIGHT

Months one through twelve. The hardest year. The causeway-building year.

You're building from nothing while fighting every old pattern that created this situation. You're changing behaviors that have been automatic for years. You're executing discipline that feels unnatural and uncomfortable.

This is the year most people fail. Not because the SOP doesn't work. Because the gap between where you are and where you want to be feels unbearable.

Months one through two: Close the gap.

You cut subscriptions. You sell items you've kept for years. You take on extra work you don't want to do. Every dollar you free up redirects to making income exceed expenses.

This is painful. You're eliminating things you enjoy. You're saying no to things you've grown accustomed to. You're working more for money that doesn't expand your lifestyle—it just closes the gap.

But somewhere in month two—maybe early month three—the gap closes. For the first time in years, maybe for the first time ever, income exceeds expenses.

You have breathing room. Not much. But the math works. The bleeding stops.

Months three through five: Build the buffer.

Same three sources. Cut waste. Sell unused items. Generate additional income. But now you redirect it to buffer instead of gap.

Five hundred dollars first. Then one thousand dollars. Money set aside specifically for emergencies. Money you don't touch unless something breaks.

This is the first real security you've had in years. A small financial cushion that stands between you and chaos.

Months six through twelve: Attack the first debt.

Anything extra—still from those same three sources—redirects to your smallest debt. Minimum payments on everything else. Every extra dollar attacks the smallest debt.

Month eight or nine or ten, that first debt hits zero. Balance eliminated. Account closed.

The amount doesn't matter. Could be eight hundred dollars. Could be three thousand. What matters is the psychological shift.

You eliminated something. You proved the SOP works. You demonstrated to yourself that you can execute a plan and get results.

One account gone. One password deleted. One less source of shame.

Most dangerous moment: Month eight.

Gap closed. Buffer exists. First debt shrinking fast.

Pressure releases. You can breathe. The constant low-level panic that's been your baseline for years suddenly lifts.

This is when most people revert.

You think: "I've been so disciplined for eight months. I deserve to relax a little. Just this once."

You buy something. Two hundred dollars you should have saved or redirected to debt. Not a huge amount. Just a small reward for your discipline.

Next month: "It's my birthday. I deserve to celebrate properly." Nice dinner. Another two hundred.

The holidays: "I can't be the only person not giving decent gifts." Four hundred on presents.

By month twelve, the gap is back. You're two hundred short again every month. All the progress from months one through eight? Gone.

That's reverting. That's Answer Two disguised as Answer One.

Defense: Your training partner catches the first reversion. They ask the hard question: "Did that purchase serve securing position or serve feeling better temporarily?"

Usually just asking the question out loud is enough. Saying it to another person makes it obvious which category it falls into.

Year one end state:

Gap closed and holding. Buffer at one thousand dollars or more. First debt eliminated. Maybe second debt partially eliminated if you were aggressive.

You're not done. You're not even halfway done. But you proved to yourself that full commitment produces results.

Foundation built. Now you can attack.

YEAR TWO: THE DEBT CAMPAIGN

Months thirteen through twenty-four. The causeway is built. Now you cross it and attack the walls.

The SOP is automatic now. You're not thinking about budgets

constantly. You're not white-knuckling through every spending decision. The discipline has become habit.

Months thirteen through twenty-four: Debt elimination.

Each eliminated debt frees up its minimum payment. That payment redirects to the next debt. Your attack power grows with every victory.

Second debt eliminated. Third debt eliminated. Maybe fourth depending on your debt load and attack intensity.

The snowball accelerates. The monthly amount attacking debt grows larger. Each debt falls faster than the last.

By month twenty-four—end of year two—roughly half your total debt is gone. Maybe more if you generated extra income aggressively or had windfalls you redirected properly.

The buffer has absorbed two or three emergencies without collapsing. Car repair. Medical bill. Appliance replacement. Each time, buffer covers it. Each time, you rebuild immediately after.

Most dangerous moment: Month eighteen.

You've eliminated multiple debts. You're making real progress. The SOP is working. You've been disciplined for a year and a half.

The deserve trap returns with more force.

"I've sacrificed so much. I've been disciplined for eighteen months. Surely I deserve something nice now."

Maybe you do deserve something. Maybe you've earned a reward.

But deserving something doesn't mean you can afford it without destroying position.

The siege of Tyre took seven months. Imagine Alexander's soldiers at month six saying "we've been building this causeway for six months. We deserve a break. Let's stop building for a while and just rest."

The causeway doesn't get finished. The city doesn't fall. The campaign fails because you took a break before completing the objective.

Defense: Call your training partner. Say out loud: "I'm thinking about spending money on X because I deserve it. Help me think through whether this serves my objective."

Usually saying it to another person breaks the spell. The deserve feeling loses power when exposed to external reality check.

Year two end state:

Gap still closed. Buffer at full target—maybe fifteen hundred or two thousand dollars now. Half your debt eliminated. Attack momentum strong.

You're over halfway through the debt elimination phase. The finish line is visible.

THE DARK MIDDLE

Before year three. After year one. In the gap between the foundation being built and the objective being reached.

This is the phase the campaign books don't talk about. Not because it isn't real. Because it's unglamorous. There's no dramatic story to tell about it. No crisis to overcome. No victory to celebrate. Just the slow grind of executing a system that feels automatic now but hasn't produced the finish line yet.

Months fourteen through twenty-two for most men. The exact window varies based on your debt load and income. But the experience is consistent.

Here's what it feels like from the inside.

The urgency from month one is completely gone. The initial motivation—the fired-up feeling from burning the boats, from taking the first action, from proving to yourself in year one that the SOP works—that fuel is spent. You're not running on motivation anymore. You've been running on momentum. Momentum has its own fuel. But momentum requires forward movement to sustain it, and in the dark middle, the movement feels invisible.

You're eliminating debts. But the big ones are still there. You're contributing to retirement. But the balance is still embarrassingly small. You're maintaining the gap. But you can't buy anything. The discipline is holding. But it doesn't feel like it's producing anything you can see or feel.

No crisis. No breakthrough. Just another month of the same protocol producing incremental movement toward an objective that still feels far away.

This is where campaigns fail. Not with a dramatic quit. With a slow drift. You stop tracking the number as carefully. You miss a training partner check-in and don't reschedule it. You make one exception that doesn't feel like an exception because the crisis from month zero feels so far away now. You round your monthly budget in the optimistic direction instead of the honest direction.

None of these feel like quitting. They feel like reasonable adjustments from a man who's been executing perfectly for over a year and deserves a little slack.

That's how Answer Two disguises itself in the dark middle. Not as failure. As slack.

Here's the tactical reality of this phase: the dark middle is where the long fight separates from the short fight. Any motivated man can run hard for eight months. The first debt eliminates. The gap closes. The system works. There's evidence. There's progress you can point to.

The dark middle has no new evidence. You're executing the same SOP that produced year one's results. But the results in months fifteen and sixteen look exactly the same as the results in months thirteen and fourteen. Small debt payoffs on debts that were medium-sized to begin with. Buffer sitting steady. Retirement growing slowly. Nothing dramatic. Nothing Instagram-worthy.

In martial arts, this is the brown belt phase. You're past white belt—you've proven you belong and you know the basic moves. You're not black belt—you haven't mastered anything yet. You're in the competent middle, where the excitement of being new has worn off and the satisfaction of mastery hasn't arrived yet. Most people quit martial arts as green belts. Not because they can't get to black belt. Because the brown belt phase is boring and their initial motivation is spent.

You're in the financial equivalent of a brown belt phase and three things carry men through it.

Evidence. That number you've been tracking every month since day one. Pull it up. Look at month one compared to right now. The gap between those two numbers is real progress. It doesn't feel dramatic from inside the movement. Measured from outside the movement, it's significant. When you don't feel progress, look at the data. The data doesn't care how you feel.

The training partner. The man who's been checking in with you since month one. He can see your progress from outside your perspective. He knows where you started. He knows what you've eliminated. When the dark middle makes the progress invisible to you, your training partner can reflect it back. That's not a small thing. That's the entire point of the training partner relationship. Call him. Tell him you're in the grind phase. He'll remind you what you've built.

The causeway. You're still building it. You can't see Tyre from the causeway. You can see the shore behind you and water in front of you and the causeway under your feet. That's enough. You don't need to see the walls of the city to keep laying stone. The work of this phase is the work of this phase. Not the work of phase three.

Keep laying stone.

Month twenty-three is coming. The snowball accelerates. The objective gets visible. The finish line appears on the horizon.

But month twenty-three only arrives for the men who kept executing through fourteen, fifteen, sixteen, seventeen, eighteen, nineteen, twenty, twenty-one, and twenty-two.

The dark middle is just months. Nothing more than that. Months that pass whether you execute or not. Execute them. Collect them. Get to twenty-three.

YEAR THREE: THE LIBERATION

Months twenty-five through thirty-six. The most satisfying year. The year the causeway reaches the walls and you breach the defenses.

Months twenty-five through thirty-three: Final debt elimination.

The snowball is massive now. Each debt falls faster. The monthly amount attacking debt has grown to include all the freed payments from eliminated debts.

Fourth debt eliminated. Fifth debt. Sixth debt if you had that many.

Month thirty-one or thirty-two or thirty-three—timeline varies based on your starting debt load—the final debt hits zero.

Last payment made. Last account closed. Every debt balance at zero simultaneously for the first time in how many years?

Five years? Ten years? Fifteen years? However long it's been, that's how long you've carried this weight.

Now it's gone.

Months thirty-four through thirty-six: Position consolidation.

The monthly payments that were going to creditors? That money is yours now. Completely yours. You control where it goes.

Half redirects to buffer expansion. Half redirects to retirement. Buffer grows to three months of expenses. Retirement contributions become substantial—maybe ten or fifteen percent of income.

Most dangerous moment: Month thirty-four.

You're debt-free. The weight you've carried for years is gone. The temptation to celebrate with spending is overwhelming.

This is the most dangerous moment in the entire timing gameplan. More people destroy their position here than anywhere else.

You think: "I'm debt-free. I can finally live a little. I've earned this."

You lease a new car. You move to a bigger apartment. You take the vacation you've been denying yourself. You expand lifestyle dramatically.

Within six months, you've recreated the gap. Within a year, you have new debt. Three years of discipline destroyed by six months of lifestyle inflation.

This is the rock bottom loop from Chapter Seven. Crisis forces change. Change creates breathing room. Breathing room triggers reversion. Reversion creates bigger crisis.

The loop tightens unless you break it by refusing to revert when pressure releases.

Defense: Maintain the austere baseline. The lifestyle that got you to debt-free is the lifestyle you keep. Just until can say it is mission accomplished. Complete the timeline before expanding lifestyle.

Year three end state:

Debt eliminated completely. Buffer at three months of expenses. Retirement contributions automated and substantial. Position nearly secured.

One more year. Just twelve more months of discipline and position is permanently secured.

YEAR FOUR: SECURING POSITION

Months thirty-seven through forty-eight. The city has fallen. Now you fortify it so it can't be retaken.

Months thirty-seven through forty-two: Position securing.

Buffer continues growing toward six months of expenses. Retirement contributions stay consistent. Expense discipline remains tight.

Nothing dramatic happens. This is maintenance-level defense after three years of offensive operations.

But these six months matter. This is where you prove that solid ground holds under normal conditions before you test it under stress.

Months forty-three through forty-eight: First year of maintenance.

Life changes. Income fluctuates. Unexpected expenses hit. Hours get cut. Car dies completely. Kid needs something expensive. Parent needs help.

These events test whether your system holds under real pressure.

If you produced real results through month forty-two, your system absorbs these shocks. Buffer covers the unexpected. Income changes trigger immediate expense adjustment to keep gap closed. You adapt without reverting.

Most dangerous moment: Month forty-six.

You've been maintaining position for almost a year. Money isn't tight anymore. You can afford things now. The stress is gone.

Small lifestyle expansions start. Nicer groceries. Better coffee. Streaming service comes back. Gym membership returns. Each expansion is small. Each seems reasonable.

Individually, you can afford them. Collectively, they recreate the gap. Slowly. Over months.

The gap that took thirty days to close in month one reopens over six months in year four. You don't notice until it's substantial. By then, pattern is established.

Defense: Monthly expense audit. Compare this month's expenses to month one's expenses. Any increase must be justified and deliberate, not automatic and unconscious.

Year four end state:

Position secured. Gap closed and holding. Buffer at six months of expenses. Debt at zero. Retirement contributions automated and substantial.

The forty-two-month campaign is complete.

ALTERNATIVE OPTION

Let me show you what Answer Two produces over the same period of time.

Months one through three: Strong start. You're motivated. You cut expenses. You build a small buffer. This is working.

Months four through six: First reversion. The discipline feels harder. The motivation from month one faded. You're still executing but not completely. Not consistently.

Months seven through twelve: Back to old patterns. Gap reopens. Buffer drains. You're not worse than month zero. You're not better either. Same position. Same stress.

Year two: Same position or slightly worse. Debt grew. Buffer didn't recover. Gap widened. The three AM calculations returned. You're carrying it alone again because you stopped checking in with your training partner months ago.

Year three: Crisis hits. Not a small manageable emergency. The big one. Job loss. Major medical. Something that requires position to absorb. You don't have position. You have the same fragility you had at month zero. Maybe worse. The crisis destroys everything. Rock bottom.

Years four through five: Now—broken, desperate, with no other options—you commit completely. You execute Answer One. But from devastation instead of from manageable struggle. You're climbing out of a deeper hole. Takes longer. Costs more. Hurts worse.

Both answers eventually require full commitment. Answer One chooses the timing. Answer Two gets forced by circumstances.

That's the difference. Not whether you'll follow through completely. When you'll act and from what position.

CAMPAIGN RESET

The forty-two month campaign assumes no major disruptions. Life doesn't cooperate with that assumption.

Job loss. Medical emergency. Divorce. Death in the family. A crisis large enough to drain the buffer, disrupt income, and force emergency operations.

When that happens—and for most men running a multi-year campaign, something will happen—most abandon the SOP entirely. Not because the system failed. Because the system got interrupted and they don't know how to re-enter it. They feel like they're back at zero. Three years of work erased by a six-month crisis.

They're not back at zero. But they feel like they are. And the feeling wins.

Here's the reset protocol for when the campaign gets disrupted. Not if. When.

Step one: Assess actual position.

You're not where you were at month zero. You cannot be, even after a major setback, because the habits you built and the debts you eliminated don't disappear when a crisis hits. Run the same six numbers from Chapter 10. Monthly income. Monthly expenses. Gap. Total debt. Buffer. Retirement contributions.

Write them down. Compare them to month zero.

Your buffer may be depleted. Some debt may have returned. The gap may have reopened. But your retirement account is larger than it was at month zero. Debts you eliminated before the crisis are still eliminated. Your capacity to execute the SOP—the habit itself—is intact. You know how to do this. You've done it for months. That knowledge doesn't disappear.

Assess honestly. You are not at zero. You are at wherever you actually are.

Step two: Identify your re-entry chapter.

The campaign sequence doesn't change. You enter at whichever battle the assessment reveals as your first priority.

If the crisis reopened the gap—income dropped or expenses spiked—you re-enter at Chapter Four. Close the gap before anything else. Same protocol. Same three sources. Same thirty-day focus.

If the gap held but the buffer was drained—the crisis hit and the buffer absorbed it, which is exactly what the buffer is for—you re-enter at Chapter Three. Rebuild the buffer. The fact that it absorbed a crisis without destroying your position is not failure. That's the buffer working as designed.

If the gap held and the buffer is intact but the crisis slowed your debt attack—re-enter at Chapter Five at whatever point you were at. Your smallest remaining debt is still your smallest remaining debt. The attack order doesn't change.

Find your chapter. That's your starting point.

Step three: Recalculate the timeline.

The forty-two month baseline shifts when the campaign gets interrupted. That's not failure. That's arithmetic.

Take your original end date. Add the number of months the crisis disrupted your execution. That's your revised end date. Write it down. Replace the original date with the new one.

You're not behind schedule. You're on a revised schedule that accounts for actual conditions instead of ideal conditions. Alexander didn't abandon the siege of Tyre because the Tyrians attacked the causeway workers. He adjusted tactics and kept building.

Your timeline extended. Your objective didn't change. Keep building.

Step four: Restart the SOP immediately.

The moment the assessment is complete and the re-entry chapter is identified, run the SOP for that chapter. This minute. This week. This month.

The longer the gap between the crisis ending and the SOP restarting, the harder the restart becomes. Inertia compounds in both directions—forward momentum builds over time, but so does stagnation.

Every day without execution makes the next day slightly harder to start.

The crisis ended. That means today is the restart. Not because conditions are perfect. Because waiting for perfect conditions is how campaigns die in the dark middle.

Step five: Contact your training partner.

Tell them what happened. Tell them your re-assessed numbers. Tell them your re-entry chapter. Tell them your revised end date.

The training partner relationship is most important at exactly this moment. When the campaign restarted feels most difficult and the setback feels most discouraging. This is when external accountability matters most. Not when you're executing well. When you just got knocked down and need someone who knows what you're building to remind you it's still buildable.

Call them. Don't text. Call.

The campaign isn't over because life disrupted the timeline. The campaign is over when you stop executing the SOP. Those are different things. One is temporary. One is permanent. You control which one this is.

Reset. Re-enter. Keep building.

CHARTED COURSE

You've seen the terrain now. The places where people lose the fight aren't where they expect—it's not month three when it's hard. It's month eight when the gap closes and it feels like the crisis is over. It's month thirty-four when the last debt hits zero and the old life starts to look affordable again.

Now you know where the cliffs are. The next chapter is about the enemy that doesn't live in the bank account.

SOP: THIS MINUTE

Write down where you are in the campaign right now.

Not where you intend to be. Where you are.

Which year? Which month? Which chapter are you actively executing?

If you're reading this before you've started, the answer is month zero. Write that down. Month zero, day one. Today's date.

If you've been executing the SOP for some time and you're reading this chapter as a reference point, write down your actual current month. Then compare it to the year-by-year timeline in this chapter. Are you where you should be? Ahead? Behind?

No judgment. Just observation. OODA loop. Observe first. That's all this minute requires.

SOP: THIS WEEK

Set up your monthly checkpoint system. Without it you're flying blind through the dark middle and won't know you've drifted until you've drifted too far to easily course correct.

Monday: Create a simple tracking document. A notepad. A spreadsheet. A page in a notebook you'll keep for forty-two months. Five lines. That's all you need.

Line 1: Month number and date. Line 2: Monthly gap (income minus expenses, positive or negative). Line 3: Buffer balance. Line 4: Total debt remaining. Line 5: Retirement balance.

That's your instrument panel. Five numbers. Measured once a month. Recorded and dated every time.

Tuesday: Fill in this month's numbers. Even if some are estimates. Even if some are worse than you'd like. Write them down. Dated. That's entry one of forty-two.

Wednesday: Identify your current dangerous moment from the chapter. Month eight, eighteen, thirty-four, or forty-six. If you're not in one of those zones yet, identify which one is coming next on your timeline. Know the cliff before you reach it.

Thursday: Confirm your training partner check-in schedule. Monthly minimum. More frequent in months one through six while the habits are forming. The schedule should be written down, agreed to by both of you, and treated like an obligation—not a casual intention.

Friday: Nothing. Instrument panel is set. Month one data is recorded. Training partner is confirmed. That's the week's work. Rest.

SOP: THIS MONTH

Run the instrument panel once. That's the monthly SOP for the entire campaign.

On the same day every month—the first of the month, your payday, whatever anchor works—pull the five numbers. Write them down. Date them.

Then compare them to last month.

Gap: Did it improve, hold, or worsen? Buffer: Did it grow, hold, or shrink? Debt: Did it decrease? Retirement: Did it increase?

Four questions. Four honest answers. Five minutes of work.

If all four are moving in the right direction, you're executing. The SOP is working. Keep executing.

If any of the four moved the wrong direction, that's your signal. Not a crisis. A signal. Run the OODA loop on that specific number. What happened? What does it mean? What's the one move this week that corrects it?

One bad month isn't failure. One bad month is data. The instrument panel exists so bad months get caught early, when a single course correction is enough, rather than late, when a full campaign reset is required.

That's how you navigate the campaign without losing the fight in the dark middle.

CHAPTER 12
ENEMY WITHIN

"We have met the enemy and he is us." - Walt Kelly

Constantinople, 1453. The capital of the Byzantine Empire. The greatest fortified city in the world.

Massive walls. Triple-layered defenses. Towers every fifty meters. A defensive system that had protected the city for over a thousand years. Dozens of sieges attempted. All failed. The walls held every time.

Then the Ottomans arrive under Sultan Mehmed II. Eighty thousand troops. The latest siege cannons. Complete naval blockade.

The Byzantines have eight thousand defenders. Massively outnumbered. But they have the walls. The walls have never been breached. If they maintain discipline and defend properly, they can hold.

The siege lasts fifty-seven days.

Day one through forty: The walls hold. Ottoman cannons batter them daily. Sections crumble. Defenders repair them at night. It's brutal work but it's working. The defenses are holding.

Day forty-one: A small gate. The Kerkoporta. A sally port built into the walls for counterattacks. Used by defenders to launch surprise raids on besiegers.

Then the worst security mistake, perhaps in the history of human warfare. Someone forgets to lock it after a raid. Or locks it improperly. Historians aren't certain which.

It's a small gate. Obscure. Easy to miss. No one was tasked to double check it. Failure one and lack of back up plan failure two.

I can just picture in the dead of night a few Ottoman scouts see and go to check the door. They push on it. It opens.

Fifty soldiers slip through. Then a hundred. Then five hundred. They're inside the walls. Inside the defensive perimeter that had held for a thousand years.

The defenders panic. They're trained to fight enemies outside the walls. Now enemies are inside. The defensive formation collapses. Chaos spreads.

Within hours, the Ottomans open the main gates from inside. The city falls. A thousand years of Byzantine Empire ends.

The walls held for fifty-seven days of bombardment. But for that one small, simple mistake they were sure to survive.

All that success lost, because someone left a gate unlocked. Because internal discipline failed at one small point. Because defenders focused on the external threat while neglecting the internal weakness.

Your financial position is Constantinople. You're building walls and defenses. Those walls protect you from external threats—job loss, emergencies, economic changes.

But walls don't fail from external pressure. They fail from internal neglect. Someone leaves a gate unlocked. Someone forgets to maintain discipline at one small point. Failed perimeter security. The breach starts small. Then it spreads. Then position collapses.

These five failure modes are your unlocked gates. The small points of internal discipline that collapse and destroy all of your efforts.

You need to know where they are. You need to check them constantly. You need to defend them with the same intensity you use to build your external defenses.

Let me show you each one.

FAILURE MODE ONE: THE PREMATURE CELEBRATION

What Happens

Month eight. You closed the gap in month two. You built your buffer to one thousand dollars by month five. You've been attacking your first debt since month six.

The math works now. Bills get paid with money left over. The constant stress that was your baseline for years suddenly lifts. You can breathe.

You think: "I've been so disciplined for eight months. I deserve to relax a little. Just this once."

You buy something. Not huge. Two hundred dollars. Something you've wanted. Something you've denied yourself while executing the SOP.

It feels good. It feels earned. You worked hard for eight months. Surely you can reward yourself.

Next month: "It's a special occasion. I deserve to celebrate properly." Another expense. Another two hundred.

The month after: "I've been doing so well. This won't hurt anything." Another expense.

By month twelve, the gap is back. Small at first. Fifty dollars monthly. Then one hundred. Then two hundred.

You're bleeding again. The foundation you built in months one through five is cracking. You don't notice immediately because it happens gradually. Each individual purchase seems justified.

Pitfall

You earned breathing room. You didn't earn reversion to old patterns.

The gap closed because you maintained austere discipline for months. Relaxing that discipline reopens the gap with mathematical certainty.

The purchases feel different from your old destructive spending. They feel justified. Earned. Small enough to be harmless.

But the pattern is the same. Spending you can't afford. Lifestyle expanding to consume available money. The gap opening because expenses rise to meet income.

Different justification. Same result.

The Timeline

First reversion: Month eight or nine. Pressure releases. First "I deserve this" purchase.

Second reversion: Month ten or eleven. Another justified expense. Pattern establishing.

Third reversion: Month twelve. Gap reopened. You're back where you started but with justifications that make it feel different.

Month fifteen: You realize you're struggling again. You're confused because you were doing so well. You don't see that you reverted. You think something external changed. It didn't. You changed.

Defense Strategy

Week one after gap closes: No changes to anything. Zero. Maintain complete discipline exactly as you've done it for the previous months.

Month two after gap closes: Still no changes. You're proving to yourself that the gap stays closed under maintained discipline.

Month three after gap closes: Small planned expansion allowed. Not spontaneous. Planned. Discussed with training partner first. One specific expense. Limited amount. With explicit decision about whether it's sustainable.

Rule enforced for six months after gap closes: Any new expense requires training partner approval before you commit. You text them. You explain what you want to buy and why. They ask: "Does this serve securing position or does this serve feeling better temporarily?"

Usually the question alone is enough. Saying it out loud to another person makes the answer obvious.

The training partner doesn't decide for you. They just force you to articulate the justification before acting. That exposure kills most premature celebrations before they happen.

FAILURE MODE TWO: THE EMERGENCY DRAIN

What Happens

Buffer hits one thousand dollars. You're proud of this. First real savings you've had in years.

Emergency happens. Legitimate emergency. Car needs eight hundred dollars in repairs. You drain buffer to cover it. This is exactly what buffer is for.

Emergency covered. Crisis averted. System worked perfectly.

But then you don't rebuild the buffer.

"I'll rebuild it next month when things calm down." Next month arrives. Other priorities emerge. Buffer stays at two hundred dollars.

"I'll rebuild it when I get my tax refund." Tax refund comes. Gets spent on something that feels urgent. Buffer stays at two hundred.

"I'll rebuild it eventually. It's not urgent right now." Months pass. Buffer stays depleted.

Pitfall

Buffer only works if it exists. A two-hundred-dollar buffer is functionally the same as a zero-dollar buffer. It won't cover the next real emergency.

Next emergency hits—and it will hit, emergencies always come—you're back to credit cards. Back to debt. Back to crisis mode.

The psychological protection the buffer provided evaporates. The knowledge that you can handle emergencies disappears. The stress returns.

You're not back to square one. You're back to square zero. Worse than square one because you proved to yourself that you could build a buffer but chose not to maintain it.

The Timeline

Month one: Buffer drained by legitimate emergency. Balance at two hundred dollars.

Month two: "I'll rebuild next month." Nothing rebuilt. Balance stays at two hundred.

Month four: Buffer still at two hundred. You've stopped thinking about rebuilding. It's not a priority anymore.

Month seven: Next emergency hits. Six hundred dollar expense. Buffer covers two hundred. You put four hundred on credit card. New debt created. Everything you worked to eliminate is coming back.

Defense Strategy

Any buffer drain—even twenty dollars—triggers immediate rebuild mode. Instant priority shift.

All extra money redirects to buffer until it's back to full target. Priority one overrides all else temporarily.

The debt attack pauses. You maintain minimum payments but you don't send extra until buffer is restored.

This feels wrong. You want to maintain momentum on debt. But buffer is the foundation. If the foundation cracks, the entire structure collapses.

Training partner asks every single week: "Is buffer back to full?" Until the answer is yes, that's the only accountability question that matters.

You don't move forward until buffer is restored. This rule has no exceptions.

Emergency happens. Buffer drains. You rebuild immediately. That's the cycle. Forever. Every time.

FAILURE MODE THREE: THE INCOME DROP PANIC

What Happens

Month fourteen. You're executing well. Gap closed for a year. Buffer exists. First debt eliminated. Second debt shrinking.

Your hours get cut. Or your overtime disappears. Or your side income dries up. Or you lose your job entirely.

Income drops twenty to forty percent overnight.

You panic. The SOP was working when you had normal income. Now income is down. The math doesn't work anymore.

You think: "I can't maintain this system with reduced income. I have to go back to survival mode."

You abandon the protocols. You stop checking in with your training partner. You return to chaotic decision-making. Emergency mode. Panic mode. React to everything without a plan.

Pitfall

The SOP doesn't require high income. The SOP requires closed gap.

Income drops, gap reopens. True. But the solution isn't abandoning the SOP. The solution is rerunning Chapter Four with the new income number.

Close the new gap. Same protocol. Same three sources. Same intensity. Different baseline number but same execution.

The Timeline

Week one: Income drops. Immediate panic. You freeze. You don't know what to do.

Week two: Chaotic decisions. You cut some things randomly. You skip bills. You borrow money. No system. Just reactions.

Month two: Position deteriorating rapidly. Gap widening. Buffer draining to cover the new gap. Debt growing because you're adding new charges.

Month six: You're worse than month zero. Income is still down but you also destroyed everything you built. Six months of chaos after twelve months of discipline.

Defense Strategy

Income drop triggers immediate Chapter Four re-execution. Same day you find out.

Run the gap calculation with new income. New income minus current expenses equals new gap size.

Cut any waste. Sell any unused items left. A benefit to selling items is the chance to hone your negotiation and business skills. It also can be a rude wake up call as to what the open market will pay for something. The next time you buy something retail or on a whim, recall back to how hard it was to sell and how much people were actually willing to pay. The offers were likely much much less than what you paid.

Temporarily reduce debt attack if necessary. Minimum payments only until gap closes.

Buffer protects you during the adjustment period. That's literally what it's for. You use it to buy time while you close the gap again. Then you rebuild it.

System adapts. Numbers change. Discipline stays constant.

Call your training partner immediately when income drops. Same day.

"My income dropped X percent. I'm rerunning Chapter Four starting today. Keep me accountable to closing the new gap."

Training partner prevents panic decisions. They walk you through systematic adaptation instead of chaotic abandonment.

The people who survive income drops are the people who adapt the SOP, not abandon it.

FAILURE MODE FOUR: THE ISOLATION RETURN

What Happens

Month twenty. You've been checking in with your training partner weekly for five months. Then life gets busy. You miss one week.

"No big deal. Just one week."

You miss another week. "We'll catch up next week."

Month twenty-two. You haven't checked in for a month. The relationship faded. You're making financial decisions alone again.

Nobody's asking if you realized your goals and what you committed to. Nobody's providing external perspective. Nobody's catching small reversions before they become patterns. Most people can barely manage their own lives, they aren't at a level where they can spare the time to truly see into yours.

Pitfall

Isolation enabled every paralysis pattern in Chapter Two. It enables them again.

You start carrying decisions alone. Making choices without external input. Rationalizing expenses without anyone questioning them. Reverting to old patterns without anyone noticing.

The reversions are small at first. Skipping one week's protocol. Making one impulse purchase. Letting one expense creep back in.

Nobody catches it. Nobody asks about it. It becomes normalized.

Six months later, you've reverted significantly. Multiple old patterns are back. Position is deteriorating.

You don't see it clearly because you're inside it. You have no external perspective checking your blind spots.

The Timeline

Week one without check-in: Feels fine. Just one missed week.

Month two without check-in: Pattern established. You're solo again. Making decisions alone.

Month four without check-in: First major reversion happens. Nobody catches it. Nobody asks. Nobody knows.

Month eight without check-in: Multiple reversions active. Position deteriorating measurably. You can't see it clearly because you're back in isolation.

Defense Strategy

Weekly check-in is non-negotiable for first twelve months.

If training partner disappears—they move, they quit, they ghost—you must find a replacement within two weeks. It would be a good idea to be on thc lookout for a "Plan B" training partner all the time, just in case.

Post in an online community asking for accountability partner. Ask someone at work. Ask someone from church or gym or neighborhood. Find someone who will ask the question: "Did you do what you said you'd do?"

You don't make major financial decisions alone. Ever. For twelve months minimum. For life ideally. Accountability and independent review will keep you on the straight and narrow.

Major decision appears. You text training partner. "I'm thinking about spending X on Y. My reasoning is Z. What am I not seeing?"

They don't decide for you. They provide external perspective. They ask questions you're not asking yourself.

The check-in can be five minutes. Text exchange works. Phone call works. In-person works. Format doesn't matter. Consistency matters.

Every week someone asks: "Did you produce what you committed to?" Every week you answer honestly.

That prevents isolation return. That keeps you visible to someone who cares about your success.

FAILURE MODE FIVE: THE LIFESTYLE CREEP

It is now year four. Whew, position secured. Debt eliminated. Buffer full. Retirement automated. Congratulations, you have proved the strength and resilience of a martial arts warrior.

Income increases over the next few years. Raises. Promotions. Better job. Whatever. You're making more than you made in year one.

Lifestyle slowly expands to match income increases. Not dramatically. Gradually. Unconsciously. Over years.

Nicer apartment in year five. Newer car in year six. More expensive habits in year seven. Better everything.

Each expansion is individually justified. You can afford it. Your income increased. Why not live a little better?

By year nine, the gap opens again. Small at first. Fifty dollars monthly. Then one hundred. Then two hundred.

You don't notice until it's substantial. By then, pattern is established. Lifestyle has expanded to consume all income growth. The margin you built is eroding.

Pitfall

How can we view it best? On its face it should be a good thing, it is an improvement of lifestyle and cash-flow has increased. So its a trap. It's understanding and planning strategic growth management.

You're not going back to your worst behaviors. Instead its an incipient slide, slowly losing the discipline that created your current position.

Expansion doesn't come with automatic defense systems as new expenses appear, you have to create new rules and regulate them live, while they are growing.

Each expansion seems reasonable in isolation. In aggregate, they recreate the gap you closed years ago.

The gap opens over three years instead of three months. Looks different. Ends at the same place.

The Timeline

Year four: Position secured. Strong foundation.

Year five: Small lifestyle expansions. Each affordable. Each justified. Moving to better apartment. Income increased. Makes sense.

Year seven: Accumulated expansions have recreated a small gap. Fifty dollars monthly. Slightly negative math.

Year nine: Gap is two hundred monthly. Still not crisis. But bleeding slowly. Back to credit cards occasionally. Debt creeping back.

Year eleven: You're fighting battles you won in year two. Different income level. Same problems.

Defense Protocol

Annual audit. Same day every year. Non-negotiable calendar reminder.

Pull all financial statements. Calculate verified numbers. Compare to last year. Compare to year one.

Questions to answer honestly:

Is gap still closed? If no, why not? What expanded?

Is buffer still at target level? If no, what drained it?

Are retirement contributions still consistent? If no, what changed?

List every expense that exists now but didn't exist in year one. For each one, ask: Is this justified and deliberate? Or is this unconscious lifestyle creep?

Justified expansions stay. Unconscious creep gets cut. Immediately. Same day.

Rule enforced annually: Income increases allocate fifty percent maximum to lifestyle, fifty percent minimum to buffer expansion, retirement increase, or investing.

One hundred percent of income increases going to lifestyle is how lifestyle creep kills position. Prevention: enforce the fifty-fifty split at every income increase. Every raise. Every promotion. Every bonus.

Calculate the increase. Fifty percent to lifestyle is the absolute maximum. Fifty percent goes to strengthening position.

The annual audit catches slow drift before it becomes fast collapse. One day per year prevents three years of unconscious erosion.

DEFEND THE GATES

Those are the five failure modes. The five unlocked gates that allow the enemy inside your walls.

Constantinople fell because defenders focused on the external siege while neglecting internal discipline. One small gate left unlocked. One small point of discipline neglected. That's where collapse started.

your footing will face external threats. Job loss. Medical emergencies. Economic downturns. Family crises. All of that is coming. You can't prevent it.

The SOP works. The math works. The failure modes in this chapter are the only reason it doesn't work for everyone who tries it—and they're all internal. The creditors aren't the obstacle at month twenty. You are. The way breathing room becomes permission. The way one missed check-in becomes two, and then suddenly you're making decisions alone again in the old patterns.

You know the five modes now. You know how they look, when they arrive, and how they pull you back toward the loop. Knowing them doesn't make you immune. It makes you faster at catching them. You can now defend the gates.

The next chapter shows you what the other side looks like—not as motivation, but as a map of what you're actually building toward.

CHAPTER 13
AFTER VICTORY

"The supreme art of war is to subdue the enemy without fighting." - Sun Tzu

Month forty-three.

You wake up. Your phone buzzes on the nightstand. Bank notification: Paycheck deposited.

You glance at the screen. See the number. Put the phone down. Make coffee.

That's it. No immediate calculation. No mental math about whether it'll cover your lifestyle. No chest tightening. No breath catching.

You check your balance because it's a habit, not because you're afraid of what you'll see.

The buffer is full. The bills are covered. The retirement deduction already happened automatically. Nothing needs your immediate attention or panic.

This is what victory looks like. Calm. Beautifully calm.

The war ended months ago. This is what peace feels like. The campaign ends. The consolidation begins. This is where most people revert—they mistake the end of intensity for the end of discipline. Consolidation isn't rest. It's converting the gains you fought for into a structure that holds them permanently.

Let me show you what the rest of your life looks like from this position.

THE ACTUAL PROBLEM

Victory is the most dangerous position in this entire campaign. Victory is harder. Because victory feels finished.

The campaign ends. The debt is gone. The buffer is full. The retirement contributions are running automatically. You completed the mission you committed to.

And then you stop.

The same way the Byzantines unlocked the Kerkoporta and forgot to lock it again after the raid. One small habit dropped. One checkpoint skipped. One month where you didn't run the numbers because everything felt fine and you didn't think you needed to.

That's the enemy in this chapter. Not a new financial crisis or new debt. Complacency.

The men who complete this campaign and then lose the position they built—and some do—don't lose it in year one. They lose it in year six. When the vigilance that won the campaign fades into the assumption that position is self-sustaining.

It isn't. Position requires maintenance although not at the same intensity as the campaign. You can't always push at 100%, sustaining allows you to dial the intensity down, and you should. In the same way a fighter doesn't stop training after winning the championship. He trains less intensely. He trains differently. But he never stops.

This chapter shows you exactly what that looks like. The maintenance SOP that holds everything you built for the rest of your life.

SOP: THIS MINUTE

The daily protocol for a secured position is this:

Nothing.

You don't think about money every day anymore. The SOP runs automatically. Paycheck hits. Buffer topped off if needed. Retirement contribution deducted. Bills paid. All of it happens without your active intervention.

You set this infrastructure up in year one. Direct deposits. Automatic transfers. Scheduled payments. The system runs without you. That's not laziness. That's victory. You built a machine and now the machine works.

Your daily life is no longer dominated by financial calculation. The mental bandwidth that financial chaos consumed for years is available now—for work, for family, for building, for thinking about things beyond survival.

That said, there is one daily habit that doesn't go away. When something flags, you act on it immediately.

Notification that a payment bounced: This minute. Find out why. Correct it.

Charge on your statement you don't recognize: This minute. Call and dispute it.

Gap calculation trending toward zero: This minute. Identify what expanded. Cut it today.

The daily protocol is zero active effort when the system is running correctly and immediate response when it isn't. Zero or immediate. No middle ground. No "I'll get to it."

That's what maintaining position looks like on a daily basis. Automated background operation interrupted only by specific signals that require your immediate attention.

SOP: THIS WEEK

Sunday evening. Same time every week. Fifteen minutes.

Open your accounts. Scan the week's transactions. Four questions.

Question one: Anything unusual? A charge that doesn't belong. A transfer that didn't execute. A balance that moved in a direction it shouldn't have. If yes, handle it now. If no, move on.

Question two: Any subscription or recurring charge that needs to go? Position secured doesn't mean spending expands unchecked. The discipline of cutting waste doesn't disappear at month forty-three. It becomes easier because you're not desperate—and that ease is the danger. Comfortable men let small expenses accumulate without noticing. The fifteen-minute weekly scan catches them before they become a pattern.

Question three: Did the paycheck allocate correctly? Buffer topped off if needed. Retirement deducted. Bills covered. Verify it happened. Systems break occasionally. Banks make errors. Weekly verification costs fifteen minutes. Missing a broken allocation costs weeks to repair.

Question four: Anything coming up this week that needs financial attention? Expense due. Payment to make. Decision to act on. Plan it now instead of scrambling when it arrives.

That's it. Four questions. Fifteen minutes. Once a week. Every week. No exceptions, no skipping because things feel fine. Things feel fine because you do this every week.

SOP: THIS MONTH

First Sunday of the month. Thirty minutes. This is your instrument panel check—the same one you ran during the campaign, now running on a secured position.

Week one: Run the five numbers. Monthly gap. Buffer balance. Total debt. Retirement balance. Net worth.

Gap: Still positive? Always. If it moved toward zero, investigate immediately. Find what expanded. Cut it same day. This is not a month-two issue. This is a month-forty-six issue and it requires the same urgency.

Buffer: Still at target level? Three to six months of expenses. If something drained it—an emergency you handled, an unexpected expense—the rebuild starts this month. Not next month.

Debt: Still zero? If any new debt appeared, name it, understand why it appeared, and eliminate it with the same priority as year one. New debt after securing position is a five-alarm signal that something in the SOP slipped.

Retirement: Still growing? Contribution still executing automatically? Balance increasing through both contributions and compound growth? If not, find the break and fix it.

Net worth: Higher than last month? Quarter over quarter increase is the proof that the position is holding and strengthening. If it declined, you need to understand why.

Week two: Review upcoming month for abnormal expenses. Quarterly insurance payment due? Property tax coming? Kid's birthday that requires planning? Parent's medical bill to anticipate? Plan the expense now instead of absorbing it as a surprise. Surprises drain the buffer. Planned expenses don't.

Week three: Training partner check-in. It may have shifted from weekly to monthly by now. That's appropriate—the intensity of the check-in matches the phase of the campaign. But it never goes to zero. Monthly minimum. You still need someone who knows your numbers and asks the question honestly. Position secured does not mean you no longer benefit from external perspective. It means the conversations are shorter and calmer. They still happen.

Week four: Lifestyle creep audit. List any expense that exists now but didn't exist six months ago. For each one: Was it deliberate and justified? Or did it accumulate unconsciously? Conscious expansion is fine. Unconscious expansion is how position erodes six months before you notice.

Every three months, expand this to the full quarterly review: Pull all statements, calculate net worth, check insurance coverage, assess major life changes that require system adjustment. One hour. Four times a year. It's the difference between maintaining position and slowly losing it while everything feels fine.

Once a year, every year on the same date—put it in your calendar now—run the full annual deep audit. Year-over-year comparison. Income, expenses, net worth, debt, buffer, retirement. All of it. Trend analysis. Are you strengthening or drifting? Income increases allocated correctly? Lifestyle creep caught and addressed? Training partner relationship maintained?

Half a day. Once a year. Non-negotiable. This audit has caught more slow-motion disasters earlier than any other single practice in this book.

WHAT DIDN'T CHANGE

The gap stays closed. Forever.

Income minus expenses equals positive number. Always. If that equation ever trends toward zero or negative, immediate correction. Same intensity as year one. This rule has no sunset clause.

The buffer gets rebuilt after every use. Every time. No exceptions. Emergency drains buffer. You rebuild immediately. Not next month. Not eventually. Immediately.

Lifestyle stays below income. Always. You can expand lifestyle when income increases, but only by fifty percent of the increase. The other fifty percent strengthens position. This rule is permanent.

Debt stays at zero. Forever. You don't finance cars. You don't carry credit card balances. You don't take personal loans. You save first, purchase second. Cash for anything that isn't a mortgage.

Tracking continues. Less frequently than year one. But consistently. Weekly. Monthly. Quarterly. Annually. You never return to unconscious spending. You maintain awareness forever.

Accountability continues. Training partner relationship might shift to monthly or quarterly. But it doesn't disappear. External perspective remains part of your life. Someone still asks hard questions occasionally.

You adapted the frequency. You didn't abandon the discipline.

That's maintenance. Different intensity than year one. Same fundamental principles.

POSITION STRENGTHENING

You're not just maintaining anymore. You're building from secured foundation instead of fighting for survival.

From this position you can begin to acquire—not things, but assets. Precious metals for safety, real estate for appreciation. The distinction matters. Things depreciate. Assets compound. Everything you acquire from this point forward should be measured by what it produces, not what it costs. The difference matters. Massive difference.

BORING WINS

There's a second way to lose everything you built.

The first way is obvious — complacency. You stop maintaining the position and it erodes. Undisciplined. The Kerkoporta left unlocked.

The second way is very common. It shows up right when you finally have surplus to deploy. It whispers that you're behind. That the boring path is for suckers. That the man who really made it — did it fast.

Gambling in its many forms. From lottery tickets to private placement investments and penny stocks. Its all gambling at a casino in one form or another. Get rich quick! So many people have done it. Play the odds and 10x or 100x your money. Why wait? Others have struck it rich, and you've heard the stories.

Walk into any casino and look at what they put on the walls. The jackpot winner. The retiree who hit it big. The kid who turned twenty dollars into twenty thousand. One story, printed everywhere, flashing on every screen. The house makes millions on the rumor and every other man in the building came looking for the same lightning. Its the trap that keeps on paying, the house. And another sucker is born every minute.

The stories are the bait. The house is the trap. And the same machine runs everywhere money gets chased: the stock that went vertical, the coin that made someone rich overnight, the trade that timed it perfectly. You never hear about the thousands (and thousands) who lost. You hear the one who won, because the one who won keeps you playing.

Truth? Real wealth is boring. Safe and boring. It's built by the man who is patient, predictable, and unexciting — the man who isn't trying to win a jackpot but to build a fortress.

My number one rule for my life is to control my time. Remember what money actually is. We looked at it in Chapter Two. Money is stored *time* — hours of your life you already spent to earn it. So follow the logic all the way down: when you lose money, you lose time. Not on paper. Actually. Every dollar gambled and lost is an hour of your life you now have to earn back. The exciting bet that goes wrong doesn't just cost dollars. It costs you the weeks and months required to replace them. It reaches into your life and takes.

It takes years to build a position. It takes seconds to lose one. The gambler at the flashy table loses in an afternoon what the boring man spent a decade securing.

So when the surplus shows up — and in years five through ten, it will — you deploy it the boring way. Slow. Safe. Into things that produce. You already made this call once, when you chose the SOP over the "perfect move" that doesn't exist. Deploying capital is the same fight. The jackpot is the "perfect move" for money. It doesn't exist either. Invest don't gamble. Or call it what it is. YOLO'ing your money away on high stakes gambling is disgraceful and sad. But at least call it gambling – *because it sure is not investing.*

SLOW and BORING wins the race. Boring isn't fun, just like a brick wall it isn't supposed to be. It is the foundation on which the rest of your life is built on. I like boring. Boring is the fortress. And the man in the fortress outlasts every gambler at the table.

THE FIVE YEAR PLAN

Year one: Every dollar had a job. Close the gap. Build the buffer. Attack the debt. No flexibility. No margin. Pure survival allocation.

Year five: You have options. Extra income can go multiple places. Invest it. Expand buffer beyond six months. Increase retirement contributions. Save for specific goals. Help family members. Multiple viable options.

That's what solid ground creates. Options. Flexibility. Choice.

The Three AM Non-Panic

2:47 AM. You wake up.

You need to use the bathroom.

You get up. Walk to bathroom. Use it. Walk back to bed. Go back to sleep immediately.

No calculations. No math. No "how are we going to cover the electric bill" spiral. No "what if the car breaks down" anxiety loop.

You wake up, handle the biological need, return to sleep. That's it.

You changed your nervous system's default state. Your body isn't constantly preparing for financial threat anymore.

The Emergency That's Just Annoying

Tuesday afternoon. You're driving home. Warning light appears on the dashboard. Engine temperature.

You pull over. Check the coolant. Low. You add the emergency coolant you keep in the trunk. Get home. Check online. Probably a leak. Could be a few hundred dollars repair. Maybe more if it's worse than a simple leak.

You call the mechanic. Describe the symptoms. "Bring it in tomorrow morning."

You bring it in. They diagnose it. Radiator leak. $650 repair including labor.

You authorize it. They fix it. You pay. Buffer covers it. You drive home.

That's it. That's the whole crisis.

No panic. No scrambling. No "how are we going to pay for this" conversation with your spouse that devolves into a fight. No putting it on a credit card and feeling sick about the new debt. No ignoring it and hoping it doesn't get worse.

Problem identified. Problem solved. Buffer used. Buffer gets rebuilt over next six weeks. System continues.

The emergency is annoying. Not devastating. There's a huge difference.

Annoying means it disrupts your day. Costs you time dealing with mechanic. Costs money from buffer. But it doesn't threaten your footing. Doesn't create cascade of other problems. Doesn't keep you awake at night.

Previous version of you: This emergency would have destroyed your month. Maybe your next three months. The stress would radiate through your house. Your spouse would be tense. You'd be short-tempered with your kids. Work performance would suffer because you're distracted by financial crisis.

Current version of you: The car broke. The mechanic fixed it. Mildly annoying. Forgotten by next week.

That's what buffer creates. Not immunity to problems. Different relationship with problems.

The Daughter's Travel Soccer Redux

Remember Chapter Eight? Your daughter wanted to play travel soccer. The cost was more than you had. You said no. You watched her face fall. You watched her try to hide her disappointment.

You sat there knowing other parents found a way. They made it work. You couldn't.

That was years ago.

This year, she asks again. Different team. Higher level. She's better now. She's been practicing constantly. This is important to her.

The cost: Still substantial. Equipment, tournaments, travel to games several hours away, coaching fees. Not cheap.

You calculate it. You look at your budget. You check your buffer. You review your upcoming expenses.

You say yes.

Yes. She can play. You'll pay cash. No debt. No scrambling. No sacrifice that destroys other parts of your financial position.

The money comes from planned allocation. You saw this expense coming. You prepared for it over previous months. When the registration deadline arrives, you're ready.

She lights up. Same excitement as years ago when she first asked. But this time, the excitement leads to participation instead of disappointment.

You drive her to practices. You drive to tournaments. You watch her play. You're fully present because you're not distracted by financial stress about paying for this.

The other parents talk about payment plans. About putting it on credit cards. About the financial stress of youth sports. You nod. You don't tell them you paid cash. You don't explain your system. You just watch your daughter play.

This is what solid ground creates. Not unlimited money. The ability to say yes to important things without destroying yourself financially.

The cost is the same as it was years ago. your footing is different. That changes what's possible.

The Brother Who Needs Help

Your brother calls. His car broke down. Transmission failure. $2,200 repair. He doesn't have it. Can barely cover rent this month. He's asking if you can help.

Years ago, this call would have created impossible tension. You'd want to help. You couldn't help without destroying your own position. You'd feel guilty either way.

Now? Different situation.

You tell him yes. You'll send the money today. He can pay you back when he's able. No rush. No pressure.

You transfer $2,200 from your buffer. He gets it within hours. Gets his car fixed. Gets to work. Crisis solved.

Your buffer drops from six months to five and a half months of expenses. Still substantial. Still protective. Just slightly lower.

Over the next three months, you rebuild it. Extra side work. Selling some items. Redirecting fifty dollars weekly. By month four, buffer is back to six months.

Your brother pays you back six months later. Half at a time. You accept it. Add it to buffer. Buffer grows beyond six months now. You have overflow.

Here's what changed: You helped him without destroying yourself. Without creating your own crisis. Without resenting him.

Previous version of you: His crisis would have become your crisis. Either you'd say no and feel guilty, or you'd say yes and put your family at risk. No good option.

Current version of you: You absorbed his crisis into your buffer. Helped him solve it. Rebuilt your footing after. He paid you back when he could. Everyone's position improved.

That's what solid ground enables. Generosity from strength instead of sacrifice from weakness.

You can't give from empty. You built full. Now you can give from overflow. Then you rebuild. System holds.

The Aging Parents

Your mother needs help. Medical expenses. Her insurance covered most of it but not all. She has a $3,800 balance. She's trying to set up a payment plan. $200 monthly. She's stressed about it. You can hear it in her voice.

You ask how much she owes. She tells you. You tell her you'll handle it.

"You don't have to do that."

"I know. I'm going to anyway."

You pay the $3,800. She cries on the phone. Not from the relief of the medical bill being paid. From realizing her kid is in a position to help her.

She helped you when you couldn't help yourself. Drove you places when your car broke down. Loaned you money when you were drowning. Fed you when you couldn't afford groceries.

Now the roles reversed. You're in position to help her.

This is a different kind of victory than buffer or eliminated debt or retirement account. This is the ability to take care of people who took care of you.

You helped her from buffer overflow. Not from stretching yourself. Not from creating stress for your family. From excess capacity.

You rebuild the buffer over two months. Back to full. System continues.

Your kids watched this happen. They watched you help their grandmother without stress or drama. They're learning: You build strong position so you can help people from strength when they need it.

That's the lesson they're internalizing. Not "be generous even when it hurts you." That's martyr thinking. They're learning "be generous from strength, which requires building strength first."

Different lesson. Better lesson.

THE COMPOUNDING EFFECT

Here's what happens in years five through ten that most people don't anticipate: the SOP starts producing results beyond what you aimed for.

Year one through four: You aimed to close the gap, build buffer, eliminate debt, start retirement. You did it. Those were your objectives. You achieved them.

Year five through ten: the SOP keeps running. But now it's operating from a completely different foundation.

Your retirement account compounds. You're contributing consistently. The balance grows through contributions. But it also grows through compound growth on the existing balance. The account balance starts accelerating.

Year one: You contributed maybe $200 monthly. Account grew by your contributions only. No compound effect yet. Balance too small.

Year five: You're contributing $400 monthly. Account balance is substantial now. Compound growth on the balance produces as much growth as your contributions. Your money is working.

Year eight: You're contributing $500 monthly. Account balance is large. Compound growth produces more growth than your contributions. The account is building itself now.

Your net worth increases faster than expected. Not because you're earning dramatically more. Because you're not bleeding money to debt service. Every dollar you earn stays yours. It accumulates. It compounds.

You start seeing opportunities previous version of you couldn't see.

Investment opportunities. Business opportunities. Ways to deploy capital that generate return.

Previous version of you: Living paycheck to paycheck. No capital to deploy. No capacity to take advantage of opportunities even when they appear.

Current version of you: Capital available. Cash in buffer. Retirement growing. No debt draining resources. When opportunities appear, you can act on them.

Your earning power increases. Not because you got smarter. Because you're not distracted by financial crisis constantly. Mental bandwidth that was consumed by survival is now available for growth.

You get promotions. You negotiate better. You take calculated risks at work. You can afford to walk away from bad situations because you have buffer. That leverage improves your footing.

The SOP system you built for defense becomes offensive weapon. Buffer protects you. That security gives you negotiating leverage. That leverage improves income. Improved income strengthens position further.

Compounding works on money. It also works on position. Strong position creates opportunities. Opportunities strengthen position further. Cycle accelerates.

MAKE THE GROUND PAY YOU BACK

You have surplus now. The compounding has started. The only question left is where it goes.

Assets, not things. This chapter already drew that line — things depreciate, assets compound, and everything you acquire from here is measured by what it produces. So start with the asset you're already standing on.

The Ground You Stand On

Own your time, and anything that controls your time you need to control. The dirt you sleep on needs to be yours – outright. So the first target is that dirt and the roof over your head. If you own it, the mortgage is the single largest, most relentless drain on your currency — a bill that shows up every month for decades and bleeds your time the whole way down. Kill it early and that drain disappears for the rest of your life. If you can't work for a period of time, you don't have a landlord or a bank to beg for an extension. You have some breathing room where you sleep to get back up and back into the fight.

If you don't own yet, this is the acquisition years five through ten make possible. Not a bigger house. A paid-off one. The ground under your feet, held free and clear, is the most boring asset there is. It's also the most defensible position you will ever hold.

Accelerate the Kill

Don't pay the mortgage the way the bank set it up. The bank's schedule is built for the bank — it wants thirty years of interest. You want your time back. Two boring (smart) moves take it.

First, change the frequency. Take your monthly payment, divide it by four, and pay that amount every week on an accelerated schedule. Whatever you can do to turn the amount of payments up will help. (Read your contract for details how.) Fifty-two weekly payments equal thirteen monthly payments a year instead of twelve. You've made one extra full payment without ever feeling it, and every dollar of it lands on principal. Smaller principal, less interest, faster kill. The math compounds against the bank instead of for it.

Second, use the annual lump sum. Again, read your mortgage contract — actually read it — and find your prepayment privilege. Most loans let you throw a lump sum straight at principal once a year, many with no penalty at all. That number is your ceiling. Build your year around hitting it. In the SOP, This Year becomes one line: save the maximum penalty-free payment and drop it on principal. Every year. No exceptions.

Stack the two and a twenty-five-year mortgage can fall in fifteen or less. The interest you save is real. The time you buy back is the actual prize — years of your life where the biggest expense you carry is simply gone.

The Retiring Vendor

Once the ground you stand on is paid off, that freed-up payment becomes ammunition. Now you make money produce.

The boring path into real estate isn't a bidding war. It's one specific seller: an owner near retirement, property owned free and clear, tired of tenants, tired of repairs. He doesn't actually want a lump sum — that's a tax problem and a reinvestment headache he never asked for. What he wants is steady monthly income and freedom from ever fixing another toilet. (Think creative here and solve whatever complication is here for them.)

You're the man who can hand him exactly that. He carries the financing. You pay him monthly, the way you'd pay a bank — except there's no bank. He gets an income stream stronger than his savings account. You get a producing asset with no bank approval, no appraisal, terms set across a kitchen table.

And don't wait to stumble onto that seller. Advertise for him. Everyone else chases listings and bids each other up. You place the ad that makes the retiring owner call you. Speak to what he wants — *"Retiring landlord? Keep the monthly income, lose the headaches. I'll buy your rental and pay you monthly — no tenants, no repairs, no lump-sum tax hit."* Run it where tired owners actually look. Let the seller come to you. And spend money on this ad. Make it professional. You want to make this work? Sell it!

Document it like the position it is — his retirement income now depends on your discipline. Note, mortgage, title, payments on record, an attorney on the paperwork. This is a contract of trust. You honor it the way you honor every other line of your SOP.

This isn't a year-one move. It's a years-seven-and-beyond move, for the man whose ground is already secured. But it's the boring engine that turns a defended position into one that pays you. Assets that produce.

Money that works. The system you built for survival, now building wealth.

NO RETREAT

After years of living in solid ground, certain things become impossible to tolerate.

You can't go back to checking your account balance with dread. Can't go back to avoiding your statements. Can't go back to that chest-tightening panic when unexpected expenses appear.

You've lived without that stress for years now. Your nervous system adapted to stability. Going back to chaos would be physically intolerable. It feels good that your default state is one of calm.

This is good. This is a defense mechanism. Your body won't let you revert to old patterns easily because it remembers how bad it felt.

You won't go back to carrying the weight alone. You have a training partner. You have accountability. You have external perspective checking your blind spots. The isolation that enabled paralysis is gone.

Trying to carry it alone again would feel immediately wrong. You'd notice within days. You'd correct it immediately.

You will not go back to lifestyle that exceeds your income. You've been living below your means for years. Lifestyle that matches your full income feels excessive now. Uncomfortable. Gross.

Your baseline expectations adjusted. What used to feel like sacrifice—living below your means—now feels normal. Expanding spending of full income would feel like self betrayal.

You can't go back to making financial decisions impulsively. You've been making deliberate choices for years. The pause between wanting something and buying something is automatic now. Impulse purchases feel reckless.

You can't go back to ignoring the numbers. You've been tracking consistently for years. Not obsessively. Consistently. The weekly fifteen-minute check is habit now. Skipping it would feel like driving without looking at the road.

All of these intolerances protect you. They make reverting to old patterns physically and psychologically uncomfortable. Your new patterns have become your default.

That's not just running on willpower alone anymore. That's identity change, you have rewired your internal subconscious programming. You're a different person now. Person who lives this way. Person who maintains discipline. Person who operates in systems and SOPs that work.

Going back would require becoming someone else. That's much harder than maintaining who you've become.

WHAT'S NEXT

You no longer lie awake with debt you can't calculate your way out of. That shift is quiet. It doesn't announce itself. You just notice one morning that you slept through the night.

The maintenance structure is what protects this. Not the intensity of year one, which you couldn't sustain indefinitely anyway—but fifteen minutes on a Sunday, thirty minutes at the end of the month, an honest conversation with someone who knows your numbers. The position holds when those habits hold.

The final chapter is about what you do with the position once it's secured. Not what you buy with it. What you build with it. Legacy isn't just about family. It's about everyone you teach. Everyone you help walk this path. Everyone who asks "How'd you do it?" and receives real answer instead of useless platitudes.

We are now at the final chapter of training. Let me show you how to teach others what you learned.

CHAPTER 14
THE LEGACY

"For us, warriors are not what you think of as warriors. The warrior is not someone who fights, because no one has the right to take another life. The warrior, for us, is one who sacrifices himself for the good of others. His task is to take care of the elderly, the defenseless, those who can not provide for themselves, and above all, the children, the future of humanity."

– Chief Sitting Bull

A "Warrior" isn't just someone who fights—it's someone who lives by a **code of discipline, preparation, and accountability.** The "Fundamental Truths" of that archetype fit hand in glove with the providers role. The (provider) person who takes personal responsibility for the safety and progression of others in their area of responsibility.

You are a provider, a warrior. Someone who steps up to provide shelter, food and comfort consistently especially when it is hard. You don't quit and you don't waiver in your responsibility. You have accepted it as your core role and you intend to deliver. I couldn't think of a better word than Warrior for such a person.

So here we are. Year five. Maybe year six. The timeline doesn't matter. You are officially a proven warrior provider.

You're at work. Break room. Making coffee. Your coworker walks in. You've known him for years. Good guy. Struggling with the same problems you used to struggle with.

He watches you for a second. Then asks: "Can I ask you something?"

You nod.

"How'd you do it? How'd you get your money situation figured out? You're different now. I can see it. You don't stress about money anymore. What changed?"

This is the moment.

Not as great a moment as when you finally you secured your footing. That was months ago. Hopefully years ago.

This is the moment you become the teacher you needed. The moment someone who walked the same path you walked asks you to show them the way. Where you can become the mentor.

What you say next matters. Not just for him. For the knowledge itself.

Knowledge hoarded dies with you. Knowledge shared multiplies. You climbed out of the hole. You know the path. Someone else in your area of responsibility now needs it.

You could just tell him to "budget better" or "save more." That's useless advice that doesn't work, that anyone can say. The advice everyone has already heard. The advice that helps no one.

You've earned this system and SOP. The protocols. The discipline. The accountability structure. All you have gleaned from this book. And you can decide who is ready to receive it from you next.

You can choose to pay it forward. And if you do, you will get something extra out of it too. Let me explain.

TEACH TO LEARN

When we take the time to explain something, we solidify our grasp of it. If we are able to teach it to people who learn differently or slower than we do, we learn even more – about ourselves and about the nitty gritty details of what we are trying to translate. Learning how to be a teacher makes us better students. But there are some caveats to assess about your potential student first.

Step One: Determine Readiness

Not everyone who asks is ready. Most aren't.

Readiness isn't about wanting better finances. Everyone wants that. Readiness is about willingness to follow through completely for however long it takes. Willingness to suffer through the discipline required.

You need to determine readiness before you invest your time.

Ready sounds like this:

"I need to change this. I can't keep living like this. Tell me what to do and I'll do it."

"I'm tired of the three AM panic. I'm tired of the stress. Show me the first move."

"I'll do whatever it takes. I trust you. Just tell me where to start."

Ready is desperation mixed with determination. Ready is rock bottom or close enough to see it coming. Ready is "I have to change or I'll drown."

Not ready sounds like this:

"Yeah, I should probably get better with money at some point. Any tips?"

"What's your secret? I don't want to sacrifice too much though. I still want to enjoy life."

"Can you just tell me what stocks to buy or what app to use? Something quick."

Not ready is casual interest. Not ready is looking for shortcuts. Not ready is wanting results without effort.

If not ready: Give them this book if you have a copy. Or point them to where they can get it. Don't invest your time yet.

Say: "Read this. When you're ready to follow through completely, come back. I'll help you then."

They'll come back when ready. Or they won't. Either way, you protected your time and energy for people who will actually use the help.

If ready: Proceed to the next step.

Step Two: Establish the Relationship

You're not rescuing them. You're not solving their problems. You're not their financial advisor or their therapist.

You're showing them the path. They walk it.

The distinction matters. Rescue creates dependence. Teaching creates competence.

The offer:

"I'll help you. Here's how it works:

First, you tell me your real numbers. All of them. Monthly income. Monthly expenses. Total debt. Buffer amount. Retirement contributions. Every cost. No hiding. No minimizing. No rounding to make them look better.

Second, I show you the exact system I used. Step by step. Battle by battle. You do it exactly as I show you. Not your modified version. Not your adapted approach. You copy what I did.

Third, we check in weekly for six months minimum. You commit to specific actions each week. I ask if you actualized those actions. That's the check-in. Five to ten minutes. Every week. No exceptions.

Fourth, you don't argue about the SOP. You don't debate whether it'll work for your special situation. It worked for me. It worked exactly as designed. You do it and see if it works for you.

Fifth, when you get results—when you secure your footing—you help someone else the same way I'm helping you. You transfer the knowledge forward. That's not optional. That's the deal.

Can you commit to all five?"

Wait for their answer.

If they agree without hesitation: Proceed to step three.

If they hedge: "Well, I don't know about weekly check-ins, that seems like a lot..." or "I want to customize it for my situation..." or "I'm not sure about telling you all my numbers..."

They're not ready.

Say: "That's okay. The offer stands when you're ready to commit completely. Take the book. Come back when you're ready."

Let them go.

You can't help someone who won't commit to the protocol. You'll waste six months on someone who acts partially, gets partial results, then blames the SOP for not working.

Protect your time. Help people who will use the help.

Step Three: Transfer the SOP

First meeting. One to two hours. In person face to face is strongly preferred. Video call if distance requires it. You need to see their face. They need to see yours.

Run their OODA loop with them:

"Get a piece of paper. Write down your numbers. Monthly income after taxes. Monthly expenses—everything. The gap between them. Total debt across all accounts. Current buffer amount. Monthly retirement contributions. Write them all down right now."

They write. They observe their reality on paper.

Most people have never written these numbers down in one place. They avoid it. The avoidance is the problem.

When they finish: "Now look at what you just wrote. What do those numbers mean? Which battle are you fighting first?"

Let them figure it out. Give them thirty seconds of silence to think.

Usually they'll say: "I spend more than I make. I need to close the gap."

Correct. Almost always correct.

"Your starting point is Chapter Four of the book. You're going to close your gap in thirty days. Here's exactly how."

Walk them through the Chapter Four protocol. Every step.

Three sources for closing the gap: Cut waste. Sell unused items. Generate additional income. All three operating simultaneously.

Show them your actions and the results if they ask. "When I closed my gap, here's what I cut. Here's what I sold. Here's how I generated extra income. Here's how long it took."

Transparency builds trust. Trust enables execution.

Then: "Your first action—before you leave here today—is to identify three expenses you can cut. Write them down. Then cancel one of them. Right now. While we're sitting here. Pull out your phone and cancel one subscription or call to cancel one service."

They do it. They complete one action with you watching.

That's their first completed OODA loop. They observed their numbers. They oriented to what they mean. They decided their starting point. They acted by canceling something.

Give them the book if you have a copy to give. "Read Chapters One through Four before our next check-in. Understand the enemy. Understand the solution. Understand your first battle."

Set the weekly check-in schedule. Same day every week. Same time. Calendar it. Both of you. Right now.

"Next Sunday, 7 PM. You text me what you committed to run this week. I ask if you completed it. That's the check-in."

They commit. You commit.

First meeting ends.

Step Four: Weekly Accountability—Months One Through Six

Same day. Same time. Every week. Ten to fifteen minutes maximum.

Their protocol before check-in:

Sunday evening, they text you what they committed to finish that week.

"This week I cut three subscriptions: streaming service, premium phone plan, gym membership I haven't used in months. Frees up $78 monthly toward closing the gap."

Or: "This week I listed five items for sale online. Two sold already for $85 total. Money redirected to buffer."

Or: "This week I attacked my smallest debt. Paid $200 extra beyond the minimum. Balance dropped from $847 to $647."

Specific actions. Specific numbers.

Your protocol during check-in:

You read their commitment. You ask one question: "Did you deliver everything you committed to?"

They answer honestly. Yes or no.

If yes: "Good. What's next week's commitment?"

If no: "Why not? What stopped you? What's next week's commitment?"

No judgment. No lecture. Just accountability.

You're not solving their problems. You're asking if they did what they said they'd do.

The question itself creates the accountability. Most people execute just to avoid admitting they didn't.

If they miss one week: Note it. Ask about it. Move forward.

If they miss two weeks in a row: Warning conversation.

"You committed to weekly check-ins for six months. You've missed two in a row. Do you want to continue or should we pause until you're ready?"

If they want to continue: "Okay. Next week can't be missed. If you miss again, we're pausing."

If they miss three or four weeks in a row: End the relationship.

"I'm available when you're ready to follow through completely. Right now you're not ready. That's okay. Not everyone is ready when they think they are. Come back when you are."

Don't waste six months on someone who won't carry through. Don't feel guilty about ending it. Your time is valuable. Your energy is limited. Help people who will actually use the help.

Some people need to hit rock bottom before they're ready. You can't rescue them from that lesson.

Step Five: Monthly Check-In—Months Seven Through Twenty-Four

After six months of weekly check-ins, the pattern is established.

Either they're executing consistently—gap closed, buffer building, debt shrinking—or they've failed and you've ended the relationship.

For those still executing: Move to monthly check-ins.

First Sunday of every month. Thirty minutes.

"Where are you on the timeline? What battle are you fighting now?"

"What's working well? What's harder than you expected?"

"Show me your numbers. Gap still closed? Buffer growing? Debt shrinking according to plan?"

"What's next month's focus?"

You're verifying the SOP is working. You're catching reversions early before they become patterns. You're providing external perspective when they get discouraged.

Around month twelve, they'll hit their first major dangerous moment. The premature celebration. Gap closed. Buffer exists. First debt eliminated or close to it. Pressure releases. Temptation to revert.

This is when you remind them: "You earned breathing room. You didn't earn reversion to old patterns. Maintain the discipline that got you here."

They listen because you've been checking in for a year. You've built credibility through consistency.

That's months seven through twenty-four. Once monthly. Never skipped.

Step Six: The Handoff—Month Twenty-Four Plus

Two years in. If they've enacted, they're self-sustaining.

Gap closed for two years. Buffer built and maintained. Debt half eliminated or more. They know the SOP. They execute automatically.

The handoff conversation:

"You don't need regular check-ins anymore. You know the SOP. You're executing. Keep going through month forty-two to complete the full timeline.

I'm available if you hit something unexpected. Call me. Text me. I'll help.

But you don't need weekly or monthly accountability anymore. You've internalized the discipline.

Your job now is to watch for someone else. Someone who asks how you did it. Someone who's ready to follow through completely.

When you find them, you show them exactly what I showed you. It will be your opportunity to teach to learn, and find new details that you will grow from as you help them.

That's how this spreads. Person to person. Each one teaching the next."

They graduate. They continue executing. They eventually teach someone else.

That's the cycle.

What You Don't Do

Don't give them money. Ever. Under any circumstances.

They need to execute the SOP and build stability through their own effort. Giving money teaches dependence, not discipline. Rescue prevents the growth that comes from climbing out yourself.

If they can't afford food this week: Point them to food banks. Community assistance programs. Government aid if they qualify. Help them access existing resources.

But don't give money. Don't *lend* money. Don't *co-sign* for them. Don't *bail* them out. All of those are a hard *NO*.

You show them how to solve their problems. You don't solve their problems for them. You have heard it before, "Give a man a fish and feed him for a day, but teach him how to fish and feed him for life."

Don't solve their tactical decisions.

They come to you: "I have $200 extra this month. Should I put it toward debt or buffer?"

You don't tell them which one. You ask: "What does the SOP say? What chapter are you executing?"

If they're in Chapter Five—attacking debt—the answer is debt. If they're in Chapter Three—building buffer—the answer is buffer.

They figure it out using the SOP. You reinforce the SOP.

This teaches them to think using a process, instead of depending on you for every decision.

Don't let them skip steps or modify the sequence.

"I want to start attacking debt but I haven't closed my gap yet. Can I do both?"

"No. Gap first. Always. Debt comes after. Read Chapter Four again. Perform the gap protocol completely. Then move to Chapter Five."

The sequence exists for specific reasons. It works in order. No modifications please.

Your job is to hold the line on sequence. Their job is to execute.

Don't mentor more than two or three people simultaneously.

You can't maintain weekly check-ins with seven people. You'll burn out. Quality matters more than quantity.

Help two people completely instead of helping seven people poorly.

When one person graduates to monthly check-ins or completes their handoff, you can take on another person if you want. Not before.

Protect your capacity to help people properly.

WHY THIS MATTERS

You reached solid ground through this system. It worked. Someone helped you get there. Training partner. Mentor. This book. Community. Something.

Now you transfer it forward.

Because knowledge hoarded dies with you. Knowledge shared multiplies across generations.

You climbed out of the hole. You know every step of the path. You know which steps are hardest. You know where people slip. You know what works.

Someone else needs that knowledge. They're standing where you stood years ago. Drowning. Panicking. Paralyzed. Running calculations at three AM that never help.

You can show them the way out by transferring the SOP and holding them accountable. By being the external perspective they need when they can't see clearly.

That's what providers do. We help people through crises we've already survived.

But we help them properly. With systems. With accountability. With discipline that builds competence.

We don't enable dependence. We create capability.

The person you help will help someone else. That person helps another. Knowledge multiplies across networks of people who all walked the same path.

Five years from now, someone you've never met will secure their position using this system. Because you taught someone who taught someone who taught them.

That's how real change spreads. Through person-to-person transfer of functional knowledge with accountability structures.

You're part of that chain now. Not just a recipient, but a conduit. A link in the transfer.

GENERATIONAL SHIFT

But teaching isn't just about helping your coworker or your friend or your brother.

The most important teaching happens inside your home. With the people watching you every day. Your kids if you have them. Your younger siblings if you're the oldest. Whoever looks to you as the model.

They're watching. They've been watching this entire time.

They watched you in year one when you were stressed and panicking and avoiding looking at your accounts. They watched you snap at people over small things because you were carrying weight you couldn't release.

They're watching now. Years later. After you've reached solid ground.

They're watching a different person. Calm where you used to panic. Confident where you used to avoid. Capable where you used to freeze.

They don't understand the SOP you're running. They're too young or they're not paying attention to financial details.

But they're learning anyway. Through observation. Through osmosis. Through watching how you handle problems and stress and unexpected expenses.

Here's what they're learning:

They're learning that emergencies are inconvenient, not catastrophic.

Car breaks down. They watch you call the mechanic. Get the estimate. Pay for the repair without panic. Without fighting with your spouse about money. Without stress that fills the house for days.

They learn: Problems can be solved. Money to solve problems can exist. Adults can handle unexpected events without falling apart.

That's not what you learned watching your parents. You learned that emergencies meant crisis. Meant fighting. Meant stress that radiated through the house and made everyone tense.

Your kids are learning different.

They're learning that wants and needs are different categories.

They ask for something expensive. Trip. Equipment. Experience.

You don't immediately say no. You don't immediately say yes.

You ask: "Is this a want or a need? If it's a want, can you save for part of it? Can you contribute?"

You're teaching them the distinction. You're teaching them that wants require planning and saving. Needs get handled immediately. Different processes for different categories.

They're learning that "we can't afford it" isn't permanent. It's situational. It means "not right now without planning" not "never and I'm a failure."

That's not what you learned. You learned that "we can't afford it" meant shame. Meant failure. Meant you shouldn't have asked.

Your kids are learning different.

They're learning that work has purpose beyond just earning money.

You talk about your job differently now. You talk about it as contribution. As building something, adding energy to the whole. The money is the result of the value you provide, not the only reason you show up.

When you get a raise or a bonus, they watch you redirect half of it to savings and retirement instead of immediately expanding lifestyle. They watch you make deliberate choices about how increased income gets allocated.

They're learning: More money doesn't automatically mean more spending. It means more choices. You get to decide.

That's not what you learned. You learned that any extra money disappeared immediately into the chaos. That there was never enough no matter how much came in.

Your kids are learning different.

They're learning that talking about money is normal, not shameful.

You have intelligent conversations about finances at the dinner table without heightened emotions and stress.

"We're saving for a bigger place. Here's how much we need. Here's how long it'll take. Here's why we're waiting instead of going into debt for it now."

"This month we had an unexpected expense. We used our emergency fund. Now we're rebuilding it. That's what emergency funds are for."

"Grandma needs help with her medical bills. We're going to help her. We can do that because we planned for situations like this."

They're learning that money is a tool. That it can be discussed. That problems can be solved through planning and discipline instead of hiding and hoping.

That's not what you learned. Money was either never discussed or only discussed through fighting. It was shameful. Secret. Hidden.

Your kids are learning different.

They're learning delayed gratification.

They watch you save for things. Wait for things. Plan for things.

You want a new car. You don't lease it or finance it immediately. You drive your current car longer while you save. They watch you make that choice. Watching you delay what you want until you can afford it without debt.

When you finally buy the car—cash, no payments—they see the satisfaction. The lack of stress. The freedom of owning something outright.

They're learning: Waiting makes the acquisition better, not worse. Debt makes things cost more and creates stress that lasts longer than the initial satisfaction.

That's not what you learned. You learned that if you wanted something, you found a way to get it now. Credit. Loans. Whatever it took. Delayed gratification wasn't modeled.

Your kids are learning different.

They're learning that helping others is possible.

Your brother calls. Needs help. Car broke down and he doesn't have the money for repairs.

You send him the money without creating any debt. From your buffer. You can rebuild your buffer over the next two months.

Your kids watch that. They see that you can help people because you built position that enables helping.

They're learning: Building security for yourself enables generosity toward others. You can't give from empty. You build full, then you give from overflow.

That's not what you learned. You learned that helping others meant sacrificing your own stability. That you couldn't do both.

Your kids are learning different.

The inheritance that matters isn't money.

You might not leave your kids a fortune. You might not leave them anything financial at all.

But you're leaving them something more valuable: Competence. The knowledge that financial problems can be solved. The discipline to use systems that work. The model of what solid ground looks like.

They're watching you run this system. They're watching you maintain discipline even when no one's forcing you to. They're watching you handle problems calmly that would have destroyed previous-version-of-you.

When they're adults, they'll face the same battles you faced. Gap. Buffer. Debt. Retirement. Emergencies. All of it.

But they'll face those battles with different programming. Different default assumptions. Different models of what's possible.

They watched you secure position. They know it's possible because they watched it happen in their own home.

That's the inheritance. That's what you're passing forward.

Not wealth. Capability.

WARRIOR LEVEL

You've reached the end of the book. Almost.

One more thing needs to be said about what "financial warrior" actually means.

It's not about being rich. It's about being competent.

It's not about never having problems. It's about having systems to handle problems.

It's not about perfection. It's about discipline.

The warrior isn't the person who never gets hit. He is the person who gets hit and gets back up. Who adapts. Who continues executing even when conditions change. The warrior is the last man standing. Knocked down seven, get up eight.

You became a financial warrior the first time you ran a complete OODA loop instead of freezing in paralysis. That was the moment. Observe, orient, decide, act. Complete the cycle. That's what warriors do.

Everything after that first loop was just repetition. Practice. Getting better at something you'd already started.

The warrior's greatest weapon isn't speed or strength or knowledge. It's the refusal to stop moving forward. Even when movement is slow. Even when movement is painful. Even when movement feels pointless.

You observe. Even when reality is ugly. You orient. Even when meaning is discouraging. You decide. Even when options are all bad. You act. Even when action seems insufficient.

Then you do it again. And again. And again.

That's what separated you from the paralyzed version of yourself. Not that you became smarter or earned more or got lucky.

You kept moving. You refused to freeze. You executed the loop regardless of how you felt about it.

That's the warrior's discipline.

And here's the final truth about warriors: The warrior's greatest victory is never having to fight.

You built such strong position that crises don't threaten you anymore. Problems happen—they always happen—but they don't destroy you. They're tactical challenges, not existential threats.

The buffer absorbs the emergency. The closed gap prevents new debt. the SOP adapts to income changes. You handle it all without panic because position is secured.

You're not fighting for survival anymore. You're maintaining position. Different kind of work. Different kind of stress. Manageable instead of overwhelming.

That's the warrior's peace. Not the absence of problems, new problems are still coming in. The wisdom and the capability to handle those problems level headed and without panic.

You earned that. Through focused performance. Through refusing to quit when it was hard.

Now you maintain it through the maintenance protocols. Weekly checks. Monthly reviews. Annual audits. Training partner still asking questions. You still answering honestly.

The discipline continues. The intensity moderates. The position holds.

That's victory. Not a moment. A state maintained through ongoing actions.

NEXT MOVES

The money will end. Whatever you build, spend, or leave behind has a finish line. the SOP doesn't. The way your daughter watches you handle a crisis—the steadiness, the fact that there's a plan and you're working it—that's what she carries into her own financial life whether or not you ever sit down to explain it to her.

What the next generation inherits isn't the balance. It's the pattern.

The model of someone who faced the numbers honestly, who built the buffer when it was hard to build, who paid off the debt in the right order, who didn't celebrate by reverting. That model is the inheritance.

You started this book in a fight you may not have known you were in or an enemy you could name. The fact that you're still reading means you're moving forward.

Welcome to the fight. I am so glad you joined us.

THANK YOU FOR READING THIS BOOK. Please help us spread the message of hope and help for financial discipline by leaving a review on Amazon or where you purchased this material. It is greatly appreciated.

QUICK REFERENCE GUIDE

Key frameworks and protocols organized alphabetically.

DEBT SNOWBALL METHOD

1. List all debts smallest to largest by total balance
2. Pay minimums on all except smallest
3. Attack smallest with every extra dollar
4. When eliminated, redirect full payment to next smallest
5. Repeat until debt-free

Why smallest first? Psychological wins maintain momentum.

DEFENSE MEASURES (Against Five Failure Modes)

1. Premature Celebration → Training partner approval for 6 months after gap closes
2. Emergency Drain → Immediate rebuild after every buffer use
3. Income Drop Panic → Rerun Chapter 4, don't abandon system
4. Isolation Return → Weekly check-in non-negotiable 12 months minimum
5. Lifestyle Creep → Annual audit + 50/50 rule on income increases

ECONOMY OF MOTION

Before any action: **"Does this serve my current objective?"**

- If yes → Do it

- If no → Don't do it

Everything serves the goal or doesn't happen.

EMERGENCY TEST

All three must be "yes":

1. **Must it happen this week?**
2. **Will ignoring it create bigger problem?**
3. **Is there no cheaper temporary solution?**

If any answer is "no," it's not an emergency.

EXECUTION SEQUENCE

Months 1-2: Close the gap (income ≥ expenses)

Months 3-5: Build $500 buffer

Months 6-33: Attack debt (snowball method)

Months 34-42: Build six months buffer

Throughout: Start retirement (2-3%, increase as capacity grows)

Forever: Maintain without reverting.

FIVE FAILURE MODES How execution dies:

1. **Premature Celebration**—Gap closes (month 8), you "deserve a break," gap reopens
2. **Emergency Drain**—Buffer drains, never rebuilds, next emergency destroys you
3. **Income Drop Panic**—Income drops, abandon system instead of adapting it
4. **Isolation Return**—Training partner fades, you carry alone again, reversions go uncaught
5. **Lifestyle Creep**—Years 4-9, slow unconscious expansion recreates gap Constantinople fell from one unlocked gate.

Defend all five.

FIVE OPPONENTS

1. **Desire**—Makes wants feel like needs
2. **Distraction**—Creates complexity through accounts, subscriptions, choices
3. **Comparison**—Shows others' highlight reels, hides their debt
4. **Fear**—Whispers reasons to wait, research more, avoid action
5. **Ignorance**—What you don't know you don't know

They attack simultaneously. Each strengthens the others.

FIVE TRAINING PARTNER QUALITIES

All five required:

1. **Fighting Their Own Fight**—Currently struggling, not coasting from past
2. **Won't Judge You**—Separates situation from identity
3. **Tell You Truth**—Reality-checks excuses and catastrophizing
4. **Hold You Accountable**—Checks if you did what you committed to
5. **Capable of Discretion**—Complete confidence, no gossip

Missing one quality compromises partnership.

FRAME

No new debt. Ever.

Emergency? Three options:

1. Negotiate payment plan with vendor
2. Temporarily reduce debt attack
3. Generate additional income

Don't add credit card debt. That breaks the frame.

KEY TIMELINES

30 Days—Close monthly gap

60 Days—Build $500 buffer

10-15 Months—First debt eliminated

42 Months—full commitment (debt-free, buffer built, retirement funded)

Forever—Maintain discipline

MENTOR PROTOCOL

Finding: Must have actual results, specific numbers, proven timeline

Using: Monthly 15-minute check-ins; come prepared; model everything; match intensity; execute suggestions exactly

Mirroring: Don't argue. Don't modify. Copy completely.

OODA LOOP

1. **Observe**—See what's actually happening
2. **Orient**—Figure out what it means
3. **Decide**—Choose your next move
4. **Act**—Execute immediately

Loop again. Speed of cycle determines who wins.

ROCK BOTTOM LOOP

1. Crisis hits → Forces change
2. You adjust → Crisis passes
3. Pressure releases → Old patterns return
4. You revert to comfort
5. Bigger crisis hits → Repeat

(Each cycle tightens. Each bottom deeper.)

Break it: Don't revert when pressure releases. Execute full 42 months.

SEVEN BATTLES

1. **Emergency You Can't Cover**—No buffer between normal life and catastrophe
2. **Monthly Math That Doesn't Work**—Expenses exceed income; structural gap
3. **Debt Trap**—Making payments but balances barely move
4. **Retirement Impossibility**—Timeline shrinks while position barely grows
5. **One-Crisis-From-Disaster Fragility**—One disruption from collapse
6. **Provider Inadequacy**—Can't deliver opportunities others provide
7. **Silent Isolation**—Carrying it alone because admitting struggle threatens identity

Fight in sequence. Each victory creates capacity for next.

SEVEN PARALYSIS PATTERNS

1. **Overwhelm Cascade**—Brain tries solving all problems at once, solves none
2. **Perfection Trap**—Research forever, execute never
3. **Wrong-Move Paralysis**—Catastrophic thinking about every action
4. **Path Invisibility**—Can see position and destination but not path between
5. **Decision Fatigue**—Depleted from small decisions; no capacity for strategic ones
6. **Shame Silence**—Can't tell anyone; isolation compounds every pattern
7. **Identity Threat**—Denial protects ego, destroys position

Break one pattern, others weaken. Start with most true.

SOP: THIS MINUTE, THIS WEEK, THIS MONTH

This Minute—One action in 10 minutes (cancel subscription, write number, make call)

This Week—Monday through Sunday protocols; multiple small actions that compound

This Month—Week 1-4 structure; systemic changes that stick beyond motivation

Repeat for 42 months across all battles.

TACTICAL BREATH

1. Four counts in through the nose
2. Four counts hold
3. Four counts out through the mouth
4. Four counts hold

Regulates nervous system. Enables movement.

The Tap Root is your single point of failure—and your single point of salvation. In any chaotic system, whether it's a failing engine or a collapsing bank account, there is one central "root" that feeds the crisis.

The Objective: You do not fight the symptoms (the late fees, the 0300 anxiety, the $450 shortfall). You find the Tap Root and you sever it.

The Diagnostic:

- Identify the Primary Leak: Where is the capital actually exiting the perimeter? It is rarely a "big" expense; it is usually a series of micro-breaches in your discipline.
- Trace the Energy: Follow the money back to the decision that released it. That decision is your Tap Root.
- Execute the Cut: Once identified, the Tap Root must be dealt with via extreme action. You don't "negotiate" with a failing system; you shut it down.

The Warrior's Rule: If you don't find the Tap Root, you are just "mowing the weeds." They will grow back by next payday. Finding the root requires brutal honesty and tactical data. Severing the root requires a Standard Operating Procedure (SOP) that removes your emotions from the equation.

THREE SOURCES

Building Your Buffer

1. Cut the Waste—Keep to strictly necessary purchases
2. Sell the Unused—Convert idle possessions to cash
3. Generate Additional Income—Temporary gigs, task-based cash

All three simultaneously. All proceeds to buffer.

THREE STAGES

1. **Copy**—Follow moves exactly. No improvisation. Repeat until automatic.
2. **Understand**—See why moves work. Adapt to situations.
3. **Master**—Natural. Automatic. Perfect execution without trying.

You're in Stage One. Execute 42 months. Then you'll understand.

TROUBLE TREE DIAGNOSTIC

Definition: The Trouble Tree is your **Logic Gate**. It is a pre-set branching diagnostic that removes "Vapor Lock" by forcing a binary choice: *Yes or No. Go or No-Go.*

The Logic:

1. The Lead Node: Start with the immediate failure (e.g., *Negative Cash Flow*).
2. The Binary Branch: Ask the first diagnostic question.

- *Is it an Income problem (Revenue) or a Discipline problem (Leakage)?*

3. The Elimination Process: Follow the branch until you hit the "Terminal Action."

- If Leakage-*then*-Identify non-essential "subscriptions"-*then*-Terminate.
- If Revenue -*then*-Identify sellable assets / overtime-*then*-Deploy.

The Warrior's Rule: Never climb two branches at once. Follow the tree to the ground. If you are "In the Box" at 0300, the Trouble Tree tells you exactly which wire to cut first.

TWO PATHS FORWARD

Path A: Choose now from current position → 42 months discipline → solid ground

Path B: Wait for crisis to force change → Execute from devastation → Same 42 months from broken position

Both eventually change. One you choose. One chooses you.

No Path C.—BURN THE BOATS

BIBLIOGRAPHY

COMBAT STRATEGY & PHILOSOPHY

Musashi, Miyamoto. The Book of Five Rings. Translated by William Scott Wilson. Shambhala, 2012.

Written by Japan's most famous swordsman in 1645. The source of "Do nothing which is of no use" and principles of non—attachment. Short, direct, applicable beyond swordsmanship. Read for strategic thinking and economy of motion.

Sun Tzu. The Art of War. Translated by Thomas Cleary. Shambhala, 2005.

Ancient Chinese military strategy text. Source of tactical retreat concepts and knowing when to defend versus when to abandon untenable ground. Read for understanding when to hold position and when to retreat strategically.

Coram, Robert. Boyd: The Fighter Pilot Who Changed the Art of War. Back Bay Books, 2004.

Biography of Colonel John Boyd, creator of the OODA loop. Explains how faster decision cycles win fights. Essential for understanding why speed of execution beats perfection of planning. Read for the complete OODA framework.

Richards, Chet. Certain to Win: The Strategy of John Boyd, Applied to Business. Xlibris, 2004.

Boyd's military concepts applied to business and life. More accessible than Boyd's original papers. Read for practical OODA loop application beyond combat.

PERSONAL FINANCE

Ramsey, Dave. The Total Money Makeover: A Proven Plan for Financial Fitness. Thomas Nelson, 2013.

Source of the debt snowball method: attack smallest debt first for psychological wins. Baby steps approach to financial stability. Read for detailed debt elimination protocols and motivation.

Robin, Vicki, and Joe Dominguez. Your Money or Your Life: 9 Steps to Transforming Your Relationship with Money and Achieving Financial Independence. Penguin Books, 2018.

Tracks life energy spent earning money versus value received. Challenges automatic spending. Read for deeper understanding of intentional resource allocation.

Clason, George S. The Richest Man in Babylon. Penguin Books, 2002.

Ancient Babylon setting teaching basic money principles through parables. "Pay yourself first" concept originates here. Short, accessible, timeless wisdom. Read for fundamental financial principles in story form.

Housel, Morgan. The Psychology of Money: Timeless Lessons on Wealth, Greed, and Happiness. Harriman House, 2020.

How people actually behave with money versus how they should behave. Stories illustrating why lottery winners go broke and janitors retire millionaires. Read for understanding human money behavior patterns.

PSYCHOLOGY & DECISION MAKING

BIBLIOGRAPHY

Clear, James. Atomic Habits: An Easy & Proven Way to Build Good Habits & Break Bad Ones. Avery, 2018.

Small consistent actions compound over time. Habit formation science. Systems over goals. Directly supports "this minute, this week, this month" framework. Read for building sustainable execution systems.

Kahneman, Daniel. Thinking, Fast and Slow. Farrar, Straus and Giroux, 2013.

Nobel Prize winner explaining how the brain makes decisions. Decision fatigue, cognitive biases, System 1 and System 2 thinking. Dense but foundational. Read for understanding why paralysis happens.

McGonigal, Kelly. The Willpower Instinct: How Self—Control Works, Why It Matters, and What You Can Do to Get More of It. Avery, 2013.

Science of self—control and why discipline depletes. Explains why motivation fades and how to build sustainable willpower. Read for understanding why execution is harder than knowledge.

Ariely, Dan. Predictably Irrational: The Hidden Forces That Shape Our Decisions. Harper Perennial, 2010.

Why humans make consistently irrational decisions. Social pressure, comparison effects, emotional purchasing. Read for understanding the deserve trap and comparison cycle.

MINIMALISM & ESSENTIALISM

McKeown, Greg. Essentialism: The Disciplined Pursuit of Less. Crown Business, 2014.

Only do what directly serves your objective. Cut everything else. "If it's not a clear yes, it's a clear no." Core philosophy behind economy of motion. Read for ruthless prioritization framework.

Newport, Cal. Digital Minimalism: Choosing a Focused Life in a Noisy World. Portfolio, 2019.

Intentional technology use. Reducing digital distraction and subscription complexity. Supports cutting streaming services and eliminating decision fatigue. Read for practical digital decluttering.

Thoreau, Henry David. Walden. First published 1854. Multiple editions available.

Classic philosophical text on simple living. Two years in a cabin with minimal possessions. Foundation for understanding austere living as strategic choice, not deprivation. Read for philosophical grounding of minimalism.

STOICISM

Holiday, Ryan. The Obstacle Is the Way: The Timeless Art of Turning Trials into Triumph. Portfolio, 2014.

Modern Stoicism applied to contemporary challenges. Obstacles become opportunities. Adversity builds strength. More accessible than ancient Stoic texts. Read for endurance mindset during the 42—month execution.

Aurelius, Marcus. Meditations. Translated by Gregory Hays. Modern Library, 2003.

Roman Emperor's personal journal. Discipline, endurance, focusing only on what you control. Written 2,000 years ago, still applicable. Read for philosophical foundation of warrior discipline.

Seneca. Letters from a Stoic. Translated by Robin Campbell. Penguin Classics, 2004.

Simple living, discipline, preparation for hardship. More accessible than Meditations. Practical wisdom in letter form. Read for Stoic principles in digestible format.

BIBLIOGRAPHY

A Note on These Books:

the SOP in this book draws from multiple disciplines: military strategy, martial arts philosophy, personal finance, behavioral psychology, and habit formation.

None of these books are required reading to execute the protocols. Everything you need is already in your hands.

But if you want deeper understanding of specific concepts, or if you're the type who learns better with multiple perspectives on the same principle, these books provide that depth.

www.ingramcontent.com/pod-product-compliance
Lightning Source LLC
LaVergne TN
LVHW040217110826
845146LV00005B/1315
* 9 7 9 8 9 9 4 2 3 3 2 1 4 *